Realities of Foreign Service Life

Realities of Foreign Service Life

Edited by Patricia Linderman and Melissa Brayer Hess

An AAFSW Book (Associates of the American Foreign Service Worldwide)

Writers Club Press
New York Lincoln Shanghai

Realities of Foreign Service Life

Writers Club Press
an imprint of iUniverse, Inc.

For information address:
iUniverse, Inc.
2021 Pine Lake Road, Suite 100
Lincoln, NE 68512
www.iuniverse.com

Second Edition

ISBN: 0-595-25077-7

Printed in the United States of America

To all employees and family members
who have served our country abroad with the U.S. Foreign Service.

Contents

Part III   Views from Abroad

Part IV   Family Life

Part V   Work and Technology

Foreword

The Foreign Service existence is highly specialized. Few professions affect so completely the life of both the employee and family members—down to such details as the type of car one drives, the food one serves and even the clothes one wears in public in a conservative country. To some degree, joining the Foreign Service is a leap of faith, both because the employee commits to being world-wide available and because at post, there are choices which are essentially made for the employee and conditions over which he or she has no control.

Less than in most existences, it is impossible to predict how many of the elements of one's life will turn out—housing, education for children, employment for spouses or security conditions. This leap of faith is more of a risk than some individuals and families are prepared to take. As one spouse commented, "Everyone has a different tolerance for risk in different areas." Thus, the Foreign Service is not for everyone.

The two editors of these collected essays are both experienced Foreign Service spouses who very wisely understood that the information and comments available in this collection are essentially lacking elsewhere. These essays are all written by people who have firsthand experience with the Foreign Service. They deal with its many aspects in a variety of ways. The tone varies enormously—from humorous and amusing to serious and dissatisfied. Each essay is informative, and above all, honest. They focus the reader on the "Realities of Foreign Service Life"—sometimes on subjects that are rarely mentioned.

The collection serves two invaluable purposes. First, for those who are considering joining the Foreign Service, it offers valuable information and insights by which to determine if the Foreign Service is a good "fit." At the same time, it is of tremendous value to those who have joined but who are still relatively inexperienced. Much has been written about the important role of accurate and realistic expectations in helping a person adapt to new circumstances. With their honesty, these essays go a long way towards helping to develop these all-important accurate expectations.

Because of the utility of these essays for both those considering the Foreign Service and for those who have joined but are still comparatively inexperienced, "Realities" has the potential to become one of the most useful and practical books on life in the Foreign Service. I highly recommend it because it has the capacity to promote and facilitate the candidate's, employee's and spouse's adaptation to what can be a very satisfying and fulfilling existence.

Mette Beecroft
AAFSW President Emerita

Introduction

As Managing Editor of the website of the Associates of the American Foreign Service Worldwide (**www.aafsw.org**), Melissa recently received an e-mail from a prospective Foreign Service Officer and spouse. They were still unsure about their choice, however, since they were having trouble imagining what their life would be like overseas. "Is there some kind of a book available about daily life in the Foreign Service?" they inquired.

Well, here it is—and we think it offers this couple and others like them an even more honest, thoughtful and realistic picture of Foreign Service life than we had originally envisioned at the launch of the project in 2001.

Our aim was to put together a collection of essays illustrating various aspects of Foreign Service life, in order to give people considering the Foreign Service a more realistic idea of what they might be getting into, as well as to help newcomers prepare more effectively for the journey ahead.

We intentionally focused on the daily lives of Foreign Service Officers and family members overseas, rather than the work of a diplomat. The latter is covered admirably, for example, by the forthcoming new edition of the book *Inside a U.S. Embassy*, published by the American Foreign Service Association (**www.afsa.org**).

In response to our appeal, submissions poured in from posts around the world, from the many professional writers within the Foreign Service community as well as from first-time authors wishing to help others by sharing their experiences. We received personal accounts of terrible hardships, light-hearted stories of unique adventures, and carefully-researched treatments of important topics such as divorce and spouse employment. We laughed out loud, or wiped tears away, as we read.

If you (or your partner) are considering entering the Foreign Service, and this book only helps strengthen your resolve to join, a warm welcome! You will find support, understanding and community from AAFSW and from all of the writers who contributed to this volume.

If the book helps you decide that the Foreign Service is not for you, we hope we have helped you avoid a more drawn-out and painful path to your discovery.

If you are already a member of the foreign affairs community, we hope you will be inspired by these stories and essays to reflection, recognition and laughter, as we were. We welcome your feedback through the website at **www.aafsw.org**.

This book is an all-volunteer effort, and all of its proceeds will support the important work of the Associates of the American Foreign Service Worldwide. We would like to express our great appreciation to all those who took the time and effort to submit their work, whether it appears here or not. There were, as always in a book of this kind, submissions we regretfully could not use because of space or subject matter constraints.

We would also like to thank Mette Beecroft and Terri Williams of AAFSW for their patience and unflagging support, as well as all of the authors in this volume for the generous donation of their work, as well as their cheerful willingness to submit to the hassles of endless e-mails and the painful trimming of word counts.

Patricia Linderman and Melissa Brayer Hess, Editors

PART I

An Overview of Foreign Service Life

The Dilemma of Choice

by Terri Williams

Are you considering a career with the Foreign Service? Living around the world is an exciting prospect, and serving your country has immense worth. There is much appeal in this profession. So, why are you lingering in making your decision? Why are you continuing your research? Here are some thoughts.

Americans seem to have a love/hate affair with choices. Compared to traditional societies, our environment offers us an enormous range of options and the need to make new decisions every day. We may choose where to attend college, whom to marry, when to have children (or not to), where to live, what kind of house to live in, what car to buy, and what brand of cereal (among dozens) to eat in the morning. Some would say we are blessed to have so many choices—others might say we are cursed.

Making choices can help us feel that we have control over our destiny. As Americans, most of us see the outcome of our decisions and any consequences, good or bad, as a result of our own actions. When our choices are not of our own making, some of us can become resentful. We can feel that we have had an element of control taken away.

However, choice is not always welcome. It can put us on an emotional roller coaster. Placing blame and diverting responsibility elsewhere can have great appeal. Also, having to make a choice with any potential for a negative outcome can be frightening. As Americans, we may say we believe in personal responsibility and accountability, but we may also be glad to let someone else take the heat. Doesn't it seem funny that we are so quick to like to blame when things go wrong, and yet so hesitant to give away the credit to others when the outcome is positive? Making choices is risky either way. There can be amazing relief when something intervenes and we don't have to make the decision.

Employees and family members in the Foreign Service must give up control in a number of ways. We prepare a "bid list" of assignments, but do not control which one is chosen. Our housing and furniture may be assigned to us. For spouses, work opportunities may be extremely limited. At the same time, however, living overseas opens up the possibility of new opportunities and new choices, requiring us to tap into our creativity and rise to a challenge. Some of us may enthusiastically try to take back as much control over our environment as we can, while willingly giving up whatever control we cannot get. In this case, the gain and loss of control is a kind of trade-off.

Also, in many of our Foreign Service posts, some of the ways benefits are dispersed may seem unfair. Americans value the idea of choices that are 'fair,' and of equal access to everyone. When that concept is violated, we may have a deep reaction. As an example, I may never have the means to live in a mansion, but I believe I should be able to make choices about where I live within my means, along with others like me. I may question the situation when someone like me has wildly different options to which I don't have access. It's easy to ask, "Why did they get the options and not me?" I can easily become resentful.

The dilemma that choice presents in the Foreign Service becomes evident when moving overseas and back home again. I remember some of our less-developed posts, which had few amenities or supplies that we had become accustomed to in the U.S. We complained about the lack of choice constantly. We asked each other, "When will oranges finally be in season?" "Where did you find laundry soap?" "Why does the State Department only have a limited choice of furniture and housing?" "Why can't I make my own travel arrangements?" "When will the next shipment come in to the Commissary?" We felt the need to stock up whenever we found the missing item, and gripe when our needs couldn't be met.

When we returned to the U.S., however, we found ourselves overwhelmed by the number of choices now available to us. Where I had been a hoarder of supplies overseas based on the worry that they wouldn't be available in the future, I now found myself trying to fill my cupboards unnecessarily. I still tend to buy in bulk out of habit. I also notice that we now spend hours and hours in research trying to find out every detail before we make any purchase. Too many choices—not enough choices. Both were something with which to contend and we found we had developed new habits in order to cope with either situation. Now we laugh about our overreacting behavior.

Making a decision about work can be a major life choice. If you are thinking about choosing work in the U.S. Foreign Service, the decision is both about the work and about the lifestyle. The corporate world, the academic world, the military world, and others all have their internal cultures. The same is true for the Foreign Service. It is a good idea to investigate the options that this environment offers, and a good idea to know yourself and what matters to you and your family. This knowledge helps to make an informed decision. That is not to say that your criteria might not change a dozen times as you go through life—they surely will. But, hopefully you'll have access to good information to help make those other decisions along the way.

Listening to the stories of others, and the choices they have been asked to confront, can make your consideration broader and wiser. If you are still deciding whether the Foreign Service life is for you, we hope the articles and personal stories that follow will help you make your choice. If you are already part of our community, perhaps the choices other people have made along the way will help illuminate your personal journey. It's all about choice, and the dilemma that choice produces in the decision-making process. Choose well!

The EFM Prize Package

by Sheri Mestan Bochantin

Congratulations! You have been selected to be an Eligible Family Member. Here are the prizes for which you are eligible:

You are hereby eligible to be shipped anywhere in the world, of your choosing or not. You have the option of bearing children (location is not always your choice).

You are eligible to receive housing that will be too small, too big, or just right. It will be furnished with standard dark wood or whitewashed Drexel or Pennsylvania House furniture. Your bed will be too soft, too hard or just right. You will receive water, though any guarantee of quantity, frequency, or cleanliness is hereby null and void.

You may or may not be awarded additional prizes in the form of giardia, dysentery, malaria, and other diseases that would cause a meltdown in my spellchecker.

You will be given multiple opportunities to purchase *objets d'art* from all world sources, and will most likely also accumulate an interesting selection of coffee mugs, paper weights and carved pencil boxes given to you as gestures of gratitude.

You will be the recipient of superficial relationships that will self-destruct in the span of an assigned tour. You will also be rewarded with numerous long-lasting friendships that will span the globe and offer refuge and cheap lodging in undetermined locations for years to come.

The eligible family member's memory bank and photo albums will be stocked with the sights and smells of other cultures, horrors of war and unidentified crawling creatures, and remembrances of a sunset atop the highest mountain peak, a school of incredible fish, and other indescribable experiences that you could never duplicate in your hometown.

You will be the target of family concern, envy, apathy, and home-cooked, artery-clogging comfort foods during all home visits. You will also have the option to enlighten local media spectators on real world events and adjust the sensationalized version viewed on a color box.

Language skills, club memberships, Scout troop leader obligations, and official-function invitations are all available for sale in the option package. The option package for eligible family member children includes the right to hate the offending employee and/or spouse for ruining their lives, but they will finally select the option to accept that they are different from other children and appreciate every worldly opportunity that was afforded to them.

As an EFM prize winner, you retain the right to revoke this package at any time, with the understanding that you will be rejecting an incredible character-building, life-changing, mind-altering lifestyle that has captivated and addicted many eligible family members before you.

Congratulations on your choice!

This essay originally appeared in the Foreign Service Journal's *AFSA News "Family Member Matters" column.*

A Foreign Service Career...in the balance

by Shawn Dorman

Pluses	Minuses
Having the chance to serve your country and make a positive contribution.	Having to endorse policies with which you may disagree.
Witnessing history in the making.	History in the making can be dangerous.
Changing jobs every few years.	Changing jobs every few years.
Having the chance to think and write about the latest world issues.	Often feeling that what you write goes into a black hole.
Traveling to amazing places.	Getting amazing illnesses.
The chance to live in off-the-beaten-path countries.	Actually living in off-the-beaten-path countries can be difficult.
Diplomats are treated great overseas.	You belong to the U.S. government 24 hours a day overseas, anything you say can be taken as an official statement, and anything you do reflects on the USG.
Wonderful colleagues, esprit de corps.	Some really bad managers.
Access to important, interesting people.	Most people want something from you.
Learning new things every day.	Things may never get totally comfortable.
You'll rarely be bored in a job.	By the time you know what you're doing, it's time to move on.
You gain a world perspective.	You no longer entirely "fit in" in the U.S., and you lose touch with American culture.

Pluses	*Minuses*
Each assignment sends you into the unknown.	Each assignment sends you into the unknown.
You could be an ambassador someday.	Your chances are pretty slim for becoming an ambassador someday.
Your spouse can find unusual work opportunities.	It's tough for a spouse to have a traditional career, and your spouse's career will always come second to yours.
You can save money living overseas.	The salary is not that great.
The lifestyle encourages a close family.	It's hard to find a spouse who will agree to FS life; you are far away from extended family and old friends, and you miss "being there" for important family happenings, i.e. deaths, weddings, births.
You'll have friends all over the world.	Your friends are always all over the world.
You'll do things you never thought you'd do.	There may have been good reasons for not doing some of those things.
Your kids will have an international perspective.	Moving every few years is hard on kids.
You'll have amazing stories to tell.	Not many people "back home" will want to hear them.
Foreign Service life is rewarding, challenging, and exciting, and it can be fun.	Very few at home will understand what it is you do.

"Expect the Unexpected"

An interview with Foreign Service spouse Anne A. Sullivan

Q: What do you feel is most important to help you feel settled and at home in a new place?

Our laptop computer helps us feel at home. After we move, we set up an Internet connection right away so we are able to keep in contact with our loved ones. (I just got a hand-held PC that I'm sure will be replacing our laptop when we move. It's the greatest!)

In my luggage, I bring framed photos to sit on a dresser and small tapestries to hang on the walls. These pack easily and can perk up the dingiest of rooms. I also like to have a few kitchen items, such as my favorite knife (in a checked bag, not a carry-on, of course!) and a good cutting board, that I know won't be in the welcome kit. I also must have my music. I always have a variety of CDs to fit any mood and a portable CD player. I also pack a few seasonal decorations (especially vinyl clings) if we're expecting to be living out of our suitcases during a holiday.

The first thing I like to do is to stock the refrigerator and pantry with some of our favorite foods. I cook a comfort meal on the first or second day. It helps us relax.

Children need special toys, games, familiar books, and comfort items. Some toys should be old favorites, some should be new. Video-tapes pack well. (Make sure a VCR will be available ahead of time, or bring one.) For some posts with APO, you can mail-order new toys or clothes and arrange to have them arrive shortly after you do. I also like to pack a craft or two to do on some quiet or rainy afternoon before the shipments arrive.

Children will benefit from exploring their surroundings. A journal can hold leaves, bark, ticket stubs, sketches, and lots of notes. Attach a roll of tape and a pen to a binder and let your child's learning take place. What was that new food called? Write it down, draw a picture, make comments.

Make a treasure map of landmarks and points of interest to find. Young children can color in each place once you have visited. Older children can write questions about each place before going. This will give the visit more meaning. For example, if you're going to a nearby castle, your child might want to find out how the castle is constructed, who lived there and when, what life was like, and what the castle is used for today. Your child might also be motivated by trying to locate a specific tree, museum piece, or dungeon. Some advance reading will provide you with suggestions. (They can treat their new school in much the same way. When was it built? Why was this location chosen? Who was the architect?)

Q: Did you ever experience a time in a new country when you thought you might never adjust?

The smog in Santiago, Chile, was stifling. I often had upper respiratory infections. I thought I'd never feel healthy again. This feeling led to frustration and anger.

Q: What helped you get over that feeling?

At the time, I was working at the International School, which was located high in the hills. The air was usually crisp and clean until late afternoon, when the smog crept upward from the city. I started focusing on how beautiful everything was in the little town next to the school. The horses played in the fields after the children went home. It was rural and peaceful.

Leaving the city on a regular basis also helped me survive. Chile is a gorgeous country. We explored the Atacama Desert, we went to the southern lake district and to the island of Chiloe; we drove up a volcano; we visited the Saltas de Lajas waterfall, and we went to the beach whenever we could. We also traveled outside Chile to Iguazu Falls. That trip was definitely a breath of fresh air.

I also made a friend who played the flute. I would go to her house after school, and we would play flute and violin duets. Maintaining a hobby was one of the best ways for me to forget about the negatives for a while.

Q: Were you ever aware of a moment when you suddenly realized you felt at home in a new country? What helped you feel that way?

I usually have that type of "aha" moment while I am driving. A few months into a posting, I realize I know where I'm going, how to get there, and where to park. Taking the initiative from the start and driving everywhere gives me a sense of control over my situation. (I've driven in some pretty crazy places, too!)

Q: What do you think are the most important ways to prepare for a new country?

To prepare for a new country, I like to read as much as I can and talk to or e-mail someone who is currently living there. It's important to know what type of electrical adapters we will need and whether we should ship our own peanut butter. It's also important to know what types of surprises we may encounter in the culture. What are the cultural faux pas Americans tend to make? What is the historical basis for current attitudes and behaviors?

When we were in Seoul, I often found myself with the baby in a front-carrier and my arms loaded with shopping bags. Getting through the narrow doorways and shopping stall aisles was nearly impossible. Yet, I was always surprised, and rather perturbed, when elderly men would push in front of me, and walk through a doorway with a grunt that indicated that I had been in their way. Finally, I learned that because Korea was based on a Confucian society, men, and elderly men in particular, did have the right-of-way. Women with children should allow men and older women to pass. Knowing this did not make carrying packages any easier for me, but at least I didn't get so upset when someone exercised his or her right to pass.

Q: What kind of support is essential?

The moves that have been the most successful for me have been those where someone was there to take me by the hand and show me everything. I was lucky enough to have that type of support for two posts. Someone was there to show me when, where, and how to shop; how to wash my produce; what brands of cheese are okay to eat; how to take a taxi; and what parts of town should be avoided. Those were the smoothest moves for me.

Having someone volunteer to watch my children while I attend the security briefing or accept and unpack my household effects (HHE) is very helpful. Yes, these things can be done without help, but it's not easy and it's not fun for the children.

Moving to a new post during the summer can be a challenge. Expect that many of the families will be on home leave or R&R. Your transition will be much easier if you take the initiative to learn about your new home.

Q: How have you come to terms with your role as an accompanying spouse?

I chose to be a teacher before my husband joined the Foreign Service. The only disadvantages to teaching at various schools around the world rather than at one school in the States is that I don't get tenure or retirement benefits. I have had rich and rewarding experiences that far outweigh the monetary gains I would have made had I stayed in one place.

Having a teaching credential has allowed me to teach elementary music and kindergarten, and to substitute in many other subjects. Having my Masters of Education was my key to teaching English literature and advanced composition at a top university in Seoul. Being flexible has allowed me to write for a children's magazine, teach courses for the Ministry of Education in Seoul, edit, write a book on Korean food, and accompany my daughter when she modeled children's clothing for big-name designers' advertising campaigns.

As an accompanying spouse, I have learned language skills, I have developed confidence and independence, I have made friends around the world, and I have gained a broader perspective than that of most people who have not left their hometowns.

I have met Alan Shepard (the first American in space), and Brian Mulroney (former Prime Minister of Canada). I have met Mikhail Barishnikov, and I literally bumped into Augusto Pinochet (former dictator of Chile, at a crowded cocktail party), and that was just one post.

We have hosted a Thanksgiving dinner for Fulbright scholars who were far away from home. We threw parties at our house that were among the most sought-after invitations for the cultural elite.

The Marine Corps Ball is an event I look forward to every October. Every post's ball is different, but no less important. In Korea, it was lavish, with red carpet, gilded mirrors, and chandeliers; in Honduras, it was held in a stucco building with a cement floor, but the vice-president of the country was in attendance. Regardless of the post, it is always a special occasion.

Q: What especially difficult experiences have you encountered along the way?

Living in a foreign country can be much harder than living in the States. In some countries the water must be filtered and boiled, and the produce must be sterilized. I have dealt with lower sanitation and medical standards than those in the United States. My husband contracted a terrible tropical illness, and I had a serious medical condition go undiagnosed for several years. Because of lower medical standards and our unique situation, I was medically evacuated and had to be separated from my husband for an entire pregnancy.

Extended-family issues will come up as well. As time goes by, family members become less interested in where you are and what you're doing, and more interested in when you're going to be present to help with such-and-such. There is bound to be some resentment as your sister gets stuck with caring for Aunt so-and-so. You may not always make it back in time when a medical emergency occurs. While I was only as far away as Honduras when my father had a heart attack, there were no flights available for 24 hours. He passed away just as my plane was landing.

Q: If you ever feel frustrated with your circumstances, what helps you feel better?

Music always makes me feel better. Whenever I'm in the throes of culture shock, I go home, turn on some dancing music, and dance away my frustrations.

Exercise helps me feel better physically and mentally, which gives me a more positive outlook on life. I can tolerate frustration better when I stay active. If there will be a VCR available when we get to post, I always pack a couple of my favorite exercise videos.

I also like to explore my surroundings. Whenever I'm feeling particularly helpless, I look for the beauty in a country. Sometimes the place truly is beautiful, sometimes I can only see beauty in a child's face, but I can always find something to help me regain my perspective.

Q: What was the hardest part about re-entry (returning to the U.S.)?

We arrived, 18-month-old in tow, just in time to see a spectacular Independence Day in our nation's capital. We felt so patriotic being there, and it was the first year my husband didn't have to work at some Embassy function on the Fourth of July. The next day, though, my husband reported to the office. My daughter and I were left to our own devices.

I was surprised at how difficult re-entry was. Yes, we had lived in Northern Virginia before, in an apartment in Ballston before we had children. That experience did little to prepare me to live in a house in the suburbs with a child. I had no Community Liaison Office Coordinator (CLO) to introduce me to others with similar interests or to tell me where the best shopping was. I had no sponsor or extended family member to help watch my daughter while I unpacked our HHE. Each day I had to ask, do I work on getting organized or do I take my daughter to the playground? Once I had confined the mess to two rooms, unless my daughter was sleeping, she took precedence.

The first few days were extraordinarily difficult. The movers had unpacked everything, as per our request, but they didn't put things out of our daughter's reach. We found china plates and crystal glasses on the floor next to the French doors, glass figurines on the bathroom floor, and bottles of toxic substances on the floor of almost every room in the house. It took several sleepless nights just to put away the chemicals and breakables. A week after moving in, my toddler brought me a bottle of bleach. Where she found it, I'll never know.

Trying to deal with everything we owned from HHE and storage all at once was another difficulty. Most people reach a point during their move when they can no longer make a decision. I certainly reached that point when the storage items arrived. I just looked at most of it and said, "I have no idea what to do with that stuff." It has been two years, and we still haven't gotten through it all.

Q: What helped you get over your challenges with re-entry?

Meeting people was a real problem. I met several parents with girls my daughter's age. Yet, once they found out we were living in the area temporarily, they became disinterested in pursuing a friendship. It wasn't until I discovered the AAFSW Playgroup that I began to feel comfortable in the D.C. area. I met other Foreign Service families who were in the same short-term situation as we were. The weekly play-groups, and our monthly Parents' Night Out, are great fora for sharing information and supporting one another.

Q: What is the best advice you have received in the Foreign Service?

The best advice I got was to "expect the unexpected". This is true in every situation, from cultural faux pas to driving. If something incongruous happens, we just smile and say, "Expect the unexpected." It's all part of our adventure.

Q: What do you wish someone had told you when you first went abroad?

Don't try to change everything. I wanted to make everything better. I had to learn that change is slow, and my way is not necessarily the best way for the people in the host country. I found this particularly true in my teaching work. Once I learned to listen and observe, to try to understand why they are doing what they are doing, I gained the local teachers' respect and, ultimately, became more effective as a leader.

Q: What is your advice on the bidding process?

Make sure everyone in the family is willing to go to every post on your bid list. Don't put a post on your list thinking that you'll never be assigned there. You might.

Q: Do you have any words of wisdom regarding the employment of household help overseas, which is a new experience for many Foreign Service Officers and families?

Always get references and have a trial period. Also, don't blur the line between employee and family. Your employees will be uncomfortable sitting at the table with you during mealtimes. They need their own space, their privacy.

Don't pay a salary that is not in keeping with the economy. It can upset the balance of the entire community. Do treat employees with respect, and they will do the same for you.

With our first maid, we felt it was necessary to inform her if we would be missing dinner. That's when a knowledgeable friend reminded us, "She's your maid, not your mother." You don't have to report to her, and you don't have to clean up before she comes.

At an office dinner hosted by my husband's boss when we were new to the Foreign Service, we were all complaining about the strange things our maids would do. The maids would fold the slacks instead of hanging them; they couldn't get the creases straight when they ironed; they messed up the shirt collars. After some time listening to all the grousing, the wise veteran host piped in, "My maid does the laundry exactly the way I like it." Wondering where he had found such a gem, and whether she had a sister, we listened for more details. He simply added, "…by someone else." That certainly put us all in our place. We have never forgotten that lesson.

Q: What have been some of the surprises you weren't prepared for?

Pleasant surprises: People. Generally, those in the Foreign Service community are very supportive. It is easier to make friends overseas than in the communities in which I have lived in the U.S. With postings lasting 1—4 years, there is no time for formalities. People just jump into friendships.

Not-so-pleasant surprises:

—A network reporter once had to stay in our house after being threatened by right-wing terrorists.
—We came home one evening to find a left-wing terrorist organization's initials scrawled on the gate to our house.

—Religious terrorists flew a plane into the building in which my husband was working (he survived).

—We had our evacuation bags packed for 3 years, knowing that we could leave at any moment.

—Learning to drive overseas was surprisingly challenging as well. In the States, I never saw anyone pass me on the right shoulder when I was getting off the freeway. Passing on the right is common practice in some countries. A driver commuting to work could witness a right turn from the far left lane, a car going backwards on the shoulder at 25 mph, a taxi driving on the sidewalk to make a right turn, and cars making five lanes out of two. Now, even though I am living in the States, I look over my right shoulder before I take an off-ramp.

—Finally, I didn't expect that it would be so hard to make local friends in some countries. Often, these people had befriended so many other foreigners, only to see them go, that they didn't want to make any more short-term friendships.

Q: How did the realities of Foreign Service life measure up to your expectations?

There are problems; there is a lot of red tape; the system is not perfect; however, it is a wonderful lifestyle with lots of great opportunities. It's every bit as exciting as I was expecting, but in ways I couldn't have imagined.

Why We Do This

1. There is never a dull moment.

2. You and your children will be first-class storytellers.

3. All your stories will be true.

4. You and your kids will be feel at home in many cultures, developing and practicing skills in observation, language, tolerance and understanding.

5. You will call many places "home," with friends, memories and special places all over the world.

6. Plain U.S. living will look rather bland and ordinary. You will live every moment in the spice of life—sweet or fiery.

7. Your family will develop the old-fashioned habits of talking together, eating together and sharing life together.

8. Your family will develop a wide-angle view of the world.

9. You will do things other people only dream of.

10. The spouse will write notes like this and, all in all, realize that choices are made, one can't have it all and what we do have is unique.

—Pat Olsen
19 years, three kids, six countries,
countless stories and a speckled resumé

A Foreign Service Journey to Marriage

by Steven C. Rice

Like many officers, I entered the Foreign Service unmarried. While enthusiastic about the prospects of the career, I had my reservations about my ability to excel at diplomacy and create the family I hoped one day to have. During my orientation class, I recall one evening in my apartment staring at my bid list. Having entered the Foreign Service with better French than Spanish language skills, I thought my first tour would present a golden opportunity to improve my Spanish. I had settled on a tour in Latin America—at least in terms of my bid preferences—and all that remained was filling the top slot. Would it be Havana or Mexico City? Castro's Cold War laboratory six years after the collapse of the Berlin Wall—and all the restrictions life in a Communist state implied—or the attraction of Mexico City and its greater prospects for social life? My career interests—Cuba would never come my way again—or my personal life? Having decided my experiences in four different U.S. time zones had brought me no closer to marriage, I opted that evening for my career and the chance to go to exotic Cuba. I was not alone in expressing interest in Havana (or Mexico City for that matter). Several colleagues in my orientation class bid on both assignments. In the end, I was given my first choice of assignment—unusual in and of itself—and headed to Castro's island.

My decision to arrive ten days before Christmas surprised my family and friends. Why not spend Christmas in the States? I had asked the same question of myself, ultimately determining that my transition to life in Havana would be easier before the Christmas holiday—when presumably the U.S. and international communities at the U.S. Interests Section would be engaged in holiday festivity—than after everyone had taken down the Christmas trees, grown tired of gatherings and resolved to lose a few pounds. The decision proved to be the right one, because I quickly met everyone at post and benefited from a very welcoming atmosphere.

The time I spent in Cuba was the most professionally satisfying of my career thus far, and I did not—do not—regret for a moment "choosing it" over Mexico City. (I have wondered, though, if by reversing the order of my bids I would have ended up in Cuba anyway.) It seemed that Cuba chose me as much as I chose it, and I shall be forever grateful for my tropical experiences, friends, and colleagues. It turns out I was also right that life in Mexico City would have been far better for my social life as a single male. Yet in Havana, I found family.

Actually, I was adopted. Hard to say today if I selected the family or if the family selected me. It was mutual, really. Granted, gallivanting about Cuba with a family whose children are not old enough to be in school may not sound fun to most single people, and I would argue that some times it was not much fun for the parents either. All the same, one family and I in particular—albeit I would occasionally loan myself out to other families, sometimes more than one at a time—found the arrangement quite satisfactory. I was able to leave Havana, which required the company of another NATO diplomat in the same vehicle, the adopted "parents" had an extra adult to help out with the kids, and the kids had a playmate. In a place without a lot of distraction, I also found playing with children provided welcome relief.

Granted, the circumstances were highly peculiar and the place unique, but my arrangement in Cuba nevertheless underscores a very important aspect of life in the Foreign Service: the need to be flexible and adaptable. If the one "supermarket" in Havana had an item you hadn't seen for a while, it might be a good idea to stock up. If the bathroom faucet leaked so badly that the water tank (on days when the city did not supply water) ran out, you might decide to shut off the water supply to the faucet until it could be fixed. (In Cuba, one did not first consider fixing the faucet.) If the most exciting museum had only Fidel memorabilia, be grateful for the diversion. And if you have the chance to head out of the country for a few days on business, jump at it. That's what I did when offered the chance to spend a couple of weeks in Caracas, Venezuela.

My time in Caracas was short, but not short enough that I left without confirming my theory that flexibility is essential to success in the Foreign Service. Compared to Havana, Caracas was paradise. The traffic lights worked; there was electricity all the time; and the city had a variety of restaurants—even McDonald's. When my watch broke (fortunately before my return to Cuba), I was able to replace it by making a trip to a shopping mall. Pretty neat, right? Well, not everyone at that Embassy was as appreciative of Venezuela's offerings. I heard many complaints while there about the lack of shopping (it wasn't Miami) and the backwardness of the place. (And to think I thought anyplace with a Big Mac and Doritos was fine by me.) Life, I was told, just wasn't the same as in the United States. No wonder, I thought—this isn't the United States. Yet I had a very nice apartment for my two weeks in Venezuela (a palace compared to what I could afford in Washington, D.C.), and a house to go back to in Cuba that was a short walk from the Caribbean Sea. What is more, the government paid the rent. Even in Caracas, a place wealthy enough for shopping malls, maids were readily available and relatively inexpensive. Is there not some value to having someone clean the house? Could I afford that lifestyle in the U.S.? Clearly, I could not. It is important when abroad to be grateful for what you have and maintain a sense of optimism. You will find the place—and the experience—all the more worthwhile.

Another bit of advice: expect the unexpected. You never know when life might surprise you. Just when the VCR is supposed to record the Cuban news (the highlight of evening television in Havana), the electricity is bound to go off just long enough before the generator kicks in to kill the VCR program. Expecting the mechanic to finish the car precisely at the agreed upon hour? Don't, unless you want to be disappointed. Looking forward to the hotel room on the beach? Someone may have forgotten to tell you that the door leading to the beach has been broken for as long as anyone can remember. You'll have to take a ten-minute hike to reach the sand on the other side of the glass. Oh, well. You have the pleasure of representing the government and people of the United States in a distant land.

Everyone, even if the local population despises American policy, will want to be your friend—en route to getting a visa. And don't bother trying to pass on the knowledge you acquired in consular training about the requirements of U.S. law. In countries where "whom you know" matters far more than the rule of law, it won't make much of a difference. In expecting the unexpected, you can count on a congressional or other very important visitor to drop in on the one free weekend you have next month. The evening you planned to do your taxes? Washington—which inevitably is on a different time zone even when the times on the clocks at post and in the U.S. capital are the same—will have some urgent request that drags you into the office. Be flexible, because it is bound to happen.

It will happen, as unfair as it may seem, more often to the new, young and single officer. You'll quickly discover that rank has its privileges in the Foreign Service, from nicer housing to the more glamorous projects in the office. Not to mention the call of family. It is one thing to be the new kid on the block. It is more alluring (to others) to find that you are unencumbered by family. "My kid/spouse is sick," or "I'm late for dinner." "Would you mind finishing this project for me once the boss has given you his final input?" It is bound to happen. Expect it. Unfair? Don't expect much sympathy; the Foreign Service prides itself on discipline and meeting deadlines.

Foreign Service supervisors, especially the best ones, will reward you for being the good soldier. I spent seven months in Cuba without permanent housing (as far away from work as you could possibly imagine) or my household effects. I made the best of it and chose to maintain a can-do spirit and good attitude. My shipment was caught up in bilateral relations and bad luck. Complaining may have made me feel good, but it wouldn't have sped up the delivery of my compact discs. (Always pack as many clothes as you can in air freight and suitcases so as not to look like you've lived out of a suitcase for months.) When it came time to assign housing—one problem was that the post did not have enough available quarters—I was rewarded. (Remember the house near the Caribbean shore?)

In my second posting, to Syria, I witnessed the passing of an era. Long-time Syrian President Hafiz al-Asad died toward the end of my tour. His son, Bashar, succeeded him. Not surprisingly, Washington was very interested in Bashar. Surprisingly, I was looked to for insights into Bashar's inner circle (thanks to my handling of the telecommunications portfolio, an area in which Bashar had been active) and ended up being the primary source of information on Bashar in the early days of his presidency. My supervisor and the deputy chief of mission also saw to it that a memorandum praising my efforts was added to my personnel file. You never know when the telecommunications portfolio might come in handy.

While at times we all feel we are wed to the Foreign Service, I have been grateful to wed a wonderful and supportive spouse as well. Perhaps it is because the Foreign Service expects so much—and calls on its newest members to pay their dues—that marriage can seem a liability. When marrying or dating another officer, the career can get in the way. Since one spouse cannot supervise another, it is best that both officers not be on the same career path. Better to have one political officer and a consular officer in the family than two economic officers. It also means that planning leave requires the consent of two sections. Not to forget that in seeking out assignments, one partner will usually have to make some sacrifice for the other. It is hard enough to find the right job in the right place for one officer, let alone two.

How about marrying a foreign national? There certainly are enough of them as you bounce from continent to continent. Beware, though, of cultural differences. Women are likely to find that foreign men are generally not inclined to follow a woman about the globe. While I know some who have been fortunate to acquire a husband and keep the career, many are not as successful. While women in most foreign cultures are more likely to accept to follow the husband, marrying a woman of another culture (or man for that matter) poses its own dilemmas.

I married a Syrian national and was very fortunate to find someone who understood my career, culture and language. Rita worked at the Canadian Embassy in Damascus and, hence, had command of both French and English. Having worked for the Canadians, she also under-stood North American culture—and the demands of diplomacy. My colleagues in Damascus were not necessarily so fortunate. One was engaged to a Syrian Muslim. The difference in religion, combined with pressures from colleagues that marrying someone outside the culture would not be good for his military career, caused them to break off the engagement.

Rita is Christian, so I had it far easier. All the same, some of my col-leagues—as highly as they thought of her—discouraged me from mar-rying a foreigner. I do not wish to imply that they did not have my best interests in mind. I only mean to suggest that such pressures can be expected if you date and/or seek to marry someone from another cul-ture. Also be prepared to obtain Uncle Sam's seal of approval on a mar-riage to a foreigner. There are forms to fill out, most of which your prospective spouse will find unwarranted, and numerous bureaucratic hoops—not to forget bureaucratic delays. In my case, I left post at the end of my tour and returned later for the wedding. Looking back on it, given some of the pressures I felt (and Rita as well) from our respective cultures, I do not regret the time apart. Indeed, it proved that we were devoted to each other and caused us to focus on the one most impor-tant thing in choosing to marry: what is best for us.

Marriage is the greatest adventure of my life. At this writing, Rita and I are expecting our first child. I would have never imagined that a boy from Wyoming would find the love of his life in Syria, but strange things do happen. What matters most in the Foreign Service are the people you meet and the experiences you have. The more flexible you are in the beginning, the greater will be the rewards in the end. In my experience, good things do come to those who adapt to the circumstances and are prepared to maximize their opportunities. Keep that in mind when the household effects don't arrive on time and you are stuck with the ambassador late at night. The Foreign Service is a journey, not a destination. Its greatest reward is the journey itself.

PART II
Moving and Adjusting

The Perils of Packing

by Patricia Hughes

Diplomatic life has been a truly moving experience. We pack and move, pack and travel, unpack, pack and move again—every few years. Each time it seem as though we pack away our very lives in all those boxes and cartons. In the meantime we exist—in limbo. Real living reoccurs only after we are unpacked and at home, whether that home be ours, the mortgage company's or on loan from the government.

Moving is not a simple process. We don't just pack up and leave with a good-bye nod of the head—it's far more complicated. And you can ignore the far-fetched notion that moving becomes easier with practice. It doesn't get easier, because each move is different.

We move from and to communities and countries that are new to us. The packing companies are never the same nor are their methods. And the modes of transport differ. The children are at different ages than during the last move. The clothing we pack varies according to the climate and social customs at our destination. Will we need overcoats and galoshes, or lightweight clothes for the tropics? Tux and tails, gowns and gloves?

The household items we take depend on what is provided by the government and on the rank of the officer. Will we need our china and sterling? Our crystal candlesticks? Should we take our lawnmower and pruning shears? What we take also depends on the availability of consumer goods at post. Do we need to stock up on toiletries, underwear and socks?

We have more possessions each time we move. Inevitably we collect and accumulate "things": artwork and glassware from Denmark, woodcarvings and crystal from Germany, pottery from Israel and alabaster from Egypt. Friends give us plaques and books as farewell gifts. Our children collect things too: model airplanes, toys, stuffed animals and dolls, tapes and discs, comic books and books of all kinds. When our relatives complain about having too much "stuff" in their basements and attics, I tell them, "You need to move!"

Before we leave Washington we have to get our home ready to rent (or sell): large repairs, small fix-up jobs, painting, window washing and carpet cleaning. We have read about and listened to the advice of real estate experts, the do's and don'ts of showing a home, how to achieve the best curb appeal, tricks to make rooms look larger. They say a home is most welcoming when an apple pie is baking in the oven, sending out a heart-warming, mouth-watering aroma. When the pie baker has other priorities, however, scented candles may have to substitute.

I was in the kitchen crushing garlic and chopping onions when one prospective renter—a foreign diplomat—showed up several hours earlier than his appointment. He must have found the aromas homey and familiar, because he wanted to rent the house immediately, with all the furniture.

As the departure date looms into sharper focus, we order extra checkbooks from our bank. We send change-of-address notices to our credit card companies, magazines, insurance providers and banks. Sometimes at this point in our preparations, we have to go to the bank for a loan to pay for the preparations.

It is important to point out that we are probably engaged in language training or area studies or spouses' orientation or the ambassadorial seminar while we are simultaneously making all the aforementioned arrangements, in addition to trying to sell our car.

Finally, ready or not, it is time to *separate*. I get the vapors when I think about that exercise. We have to separate our belongings into several categories: household effects, which usually travel by sea; air freight, which we hope will arrive within a month; luggage that will travel with us. If we're leaving Washington, we separate furniture and other items that will stay behind in storage. If we're abroad we segregate our things from those that remain in the house because they belong to the government. If we have a student going off to college, we arrange for an additional shipment.

The first time we packed to go overseas I was truly a novice and I believed that all moving company employees were experts. I didn't pay an iota of attention to the nice young man who packed the portable typewriter on top of the stemmed glasses. I also didn't notice the box of talcum powder he put unwrapped on top of the typewriter. Several months later when I opened the box—and cleaned up the mess—I realized I would have to be more observant the next time we moved.

I tried. Unfortunately, I missed the can of olive oil that clung to the far corner of a kitchen shelf. It was retrieved by one of the packers. By the time our shipment reached post the oil had leaked out and mixed disgustingly with the strawberry jam that had oozed from its broken jar. During the next move, I judiciously set the dish of butter on top of the refrigerator—out of reach, I thought. Not so. The butter went into a box and sailed the Atlantic with the kitchenware.

No matter how diligent and observant we have learned to be on moving day, the strangest things happen. Our wastebaskets have been packed, still full of trash. Friends told us about ashtrays wrapped up with cigarette butts in them. Someone's roasting pan disappeared from the stovetop. Inside was the smoked ham that was intended for supper. By the time the ham crossed the ocean, it was no longer fit for supper.

My shoes have been squashed and misshapen from heavy items that were piled on top of them in the cartons. Leather handbags were thrown in, unwrapped, among the shoes and boots. One summer the purses stuck together because of the heat—pieces of black patent leather melded with beige and gray. Now I keep my shoes in their original boxes and I put my purses in pillowcases. No matter how our clothes are packed—folded, laid straight in long boxes or hung in special wardrobes—they always arrive in a crumpled mass.

There is no choice but to put our possessions in the care of a packing and moving company, so we have to be trusting and prudent at the same time. By keeping a keen eye—several eyes if possible—on the packers, we may discourage petty pilfering. By pointing out fragile and delicate items, we may ensure safer handling. By hand-carrying our valuables, we always know where they are. And we cross our fingers a lot.

But mishaps still happen. Furniture gets nicked, scraped and scratched. Dishes are chipped, cracked and broken. Small items like lids, corks, thimbles and screwdrivers are lost. Figurines, silver and jewelry disappear. And there is mildew.

The worst damage suffered by our possessions occurred in a storage facility. Moisture in the warehouse permeated our dining room and bedroom furniture and our cherry wood desk. Drawers were stuck, some shut and some open. Mattresses were damp and green with mold. Cartons of blankets and pillows smelled like wet dogs. Small wooden items—cheese boards, spice racks, salad bowls—were sprouting fuzz. Leather boots were spotted with fungi. The covers fell off albums, and photographs stuck together as if they'd been glued.

It was a cold November day when the truckload of mildew arrived. It was raining and our furnace refused to start. As the mold spores multiplied, so did the odor. Our sinuses hurt, our noses ran and our heads pounded as we scrubbed with bleach and detergent and baking soda. What a mess.

We pack our own suitcases, but once they are hefted onto the conveyer belt at the airport, we lose control over those too. I've lost count of how many of our bags have been damaged along the way. Or lost. Keeping track of the family's luggage was a mathematical challenge when our children were with us. A home-leave trip required six suitcases and a diaper bag. When we were on transfer we needed at least eight pieces of luggage. Then there are the carry-on bags, plus a briefcase and my enormous purse. Depending on the season, we have also lugged coats, hats, scarves, mittens and umbrellas.

In my carry-on bag I put toothbrushes, a hairbrush, cosmetics and of course the jewelry. And due to previous misfortunes I now carry "spare pairs"—underwear and pantyhose. I always take food; a snack is essential in case the airplane is stuck on the runway for a couple of hours after we have boarded. Those are just the essentials. If well-wishers at the airport give us farewell gifts, we have to carry another bag.

People who are relatively stationary in their living arrangements often ask me, "How do you like moving so often?" My answer depends on *when* I am asked: I have just moved, I am preparing to move, or I am well settled in. The latter situation produces the most positive response.

Dreaming of Foreign Service Life

by Jan Fischer Bachman

I am on a bus, traveling down a wide street lined with houses and big shade trees. I don't recognize anything, although the type of place looks familiar. I find myself calling to the driver, "Could you drop me off, please?"

I hear the quiet murmur of snide amusement: "How quaint!"

"She thinks the bus will take her home."

I pretend not to notice. I know that we haven't passed my house. I am going to get off the bus and walk back along the street. I hope, by some kind of miracle, that if I stroll along the street in the willful act of belonging, that I will, in fact, arrive home.

I don't know what home looks like.

As I descend the bus steps, my two-year-old daughter, Emma, wakes me.

"I want breakfast."

I roll out of bed under protest. It is 6:50 and still dark. My husband, Brian, is in Virginia speaking at a conference on Caribbean issues. It doesn't make much of a difference to this part of our day. Normally at this time, he has already left for work. They say that after 7:10 the roads into Nassau are impossible. I hope to never find out firsthand.

Brian began working as the Political and Economic Chief at the U.S. Embassy here in the Bahamas three months ago. He has slipped very easily into his role, thriving in spite of a series of major and minor crises. I am finding it more difficult to find my place since I cannot legally work without surmounting expensive bureaucratic hurdles. I am not worried about that this early in the morning. I am worried about finding something vaguely nutritious that will fit in an insulated lunch pack. Even in 90-degree heat, school lunches go into outdoor cubbies. Brown paper bags are out of the question, unless you're aiming for half-grilled cheese sandwiches.

For breakfast, Bahamians eat tuna or grits or "souse," stew made of chicken or fish. Grace and Emma have not learned to face tuna before noon. They are flexible in their habits, however, happily breakfasting on any cereal with sugar as a primary ingredient.

Bahamian supermarkets are obligingly filled with U.S. products. If you want local fruits or vegetables, however, you have to buy them from the Fruit and Vegetable Exchange, located under the bridge to Paradise Island, or from street vendors—or obtain them as gifts from friends, the method most Bahamians seem to use. My first week in the Bahamas, I tried to show my desire to adapt by buying a bag of grits. I made them for breakfast on and off for two weeks. I was the only one who would eat them. Then I got tired of washing the pans. Dishwashers are not very common here, and our house is no exception.

It is a beautiful drive to the school. If there is time, I make the five-mile trip around the eastern end of the island along the ocean. In some places the houses hide the view, but in other places the seascapes are spectacular. There are seldom any cars since no one seems to want to take the extra two minutes to go all the way around the point instead of through the suburbs. Everyday life is not *that* relaxed on this tropical island.

Just before the school turnoff we see Yamacraw Beach, a thin strip of yellow sand beneath shaggy palms and native pine trees. Yamacraw is not a tourist destination. The only access is along a rutted dirt track lined with messy heaps of overflowing black trash bags. However, the crystalline water extends knee-deep for hundreds of yards. On a sunny day—in other words, most days—the water is as warm as the most relaxing bath, and the reassuring depth makes it easy to keep track of otter-imitating, water-worshipping children.

Back at home, our Haitian gardener Gayle has arrived. He came with the house, more or less. He helped our landlady try to get half a lawn established during the eight months she lived in the house. It took us weeks to decide to re-hire him for the one day a week that he comes. We are used to the do-it-yourself mentality. However, a half-acre of tough grass and weeds has defied our gardening efforts. Personally, I am not that comfortable working with a machete, here called a cutlass, in Caribbean pirate fashion. Not much else works on rampant, rainy-season weeds.

Gayle does not speak a lot of English and I don't know a word of Haitian Creole. Normally when I try to make a new request, he says something that sounds like, "Yes, Mom," and then he keeps on working on whatever he was doing before I interrupted him. Today is a mowing day, but I ask him to pull a few weeds in the area we have designated as a vegetable garden. The house was built just a year ago and a third of the yard is still sand. The girls collect shells on what they call "our beach." Strangely enough, plants grow beautifully in what looks like a total lack of soil. There is probably a profound lesson here somewhere, but right now I would just like to see fewer weeds.

Today is not one of Emma's preschool days, so she is going with me to an eye appointment. Before we leave I quickly check e-mail. As long as we have electricity, the cable modem service is fantastic. Today I see notes from an online writers' group and "newsletters" from two merchants. It is tempting to shop online when local prices are so high. One friend writes a brief greeting. Sometimes it's hard to answer the personal messages, because I cope very well with my current life by ignoring the fact that I used to have a different one. Here's a job announcement from the Embassy. I could earn all of $15 per hour if I am very qualified! Great! I could earn $150 to 250 per hour locally playing the violin professionally if there were a bilateral work agreement. Unfortunately, that has not even entered the preliminary planning stage.

Off to get some prescription sunglasses. I also need contact lenses, since I recently ruined one trying to put it away by candlelight. Sometimes the power doesn't go out for weeks. Sometimes it is off for hours on end. Every now and then I am lucky enough to lose electricity just when I most want to procrastinate. We have a gas stove, so it is still possible to make a good cup of tea—as long as the tiny ghost ants haven't gotten into the tea kettle, one of their favorite hiding places.

The optometrist turns out to be a fellow late-arriving mother from Grace's school. It is a small island. We talk about children and work. She gives me a discount on my eye exam. Everyone is very kind to Emma, who eats her packed lunch and puts far too many finger marks on the plate glass storefront.

Back at home, I quickly heat up some soup and leftover pasta for Gayle. It is 1:20, which is quite late for lunch. I am never entirely sure what is supposed to happen about lunch. Gayle usually disappears for an hour at noon. For all I know, he is eating lunch. However, I have been told that if someone works at your house all day, you need to provide lunch. Maybe Gayle eats two lunches on Thursdays. The plate has always come back empty. I notice that the weeds are gone. This is a first! Maybe I am finally learning how to communicate.

Emma and I play "Pretty Princess," a game to which I am opposed in principle. A friend calls to invite us for supper since Brian is away. She gives me a telephone number I have been trying to find, that of a nearby piano teacher. I give the piano teacher a quick call, and we arrange to meet up to play some duets.

Emma and I pick up Grace from school. It suddenly pours with rain. Emma wants to be carried. We all talk, normal after-school kind of talk. We arrive home. The pink house still surprises me. It was beautifully designed, with a circular drive in front and white columns. It looks completely out of place in the treeless yard. The chain link fence and razor wire don't look right either. This is a high-crime post, but I still feel trapped by the iron bars on the windows.

Grace and Emma decide to design a boat with craft materials. I find them a chopstick for a mast. We go to our friends' house. Lance, the husband, agrees to watch my two girls along with his own while Christie and I go for a walk. Christie carries her dog-whacking stick. She is an animal activist, but the stray dogs don't always recognize that fact. I tell her about this morning's dream.

"I guess you are feeling lost," she says.

I wonder about that term. People trying to create a new life in a new country often describe themselves as feeling lost. When I am actually physically lost, really lost, I feel anxious, irritated, sometimes terrified. I do not feel lost now. What I mostly feel is sad. I walk around feeling a constant, low-grade sadness, a sadness I can ignore for hours on end, but which never really leaves completely.

I get the girls ready for bed. We try to call Brian in Virginia, but he is not back at the hotel yet. I make a cup of tea. I look at the pile of dishes. I ignore them. I read a few pages of a book. I remember that I need to answer an e-mail from someone who took over one of my previous editing jobs, so I head for my office, just off the kitchen. It is a wonderful luxury to have my own office. I write a quick critique for my online writers' group. I finish an article. It is too late, but right now I have very little time for my own projects. I go to bed, hoping that tonight I'll dream about nothing more than wave after wave of crystal clear, turquoise water.

One Thing At A Time

by Francesca Kelly

How quickly one forgets. We're less than a week at our new overseas posting, and it's all coming back to me now: how it is that first week in a completely new country, city, job, language, life. I'd forgotten that no matter how fascinating a place you're in, it's always rough going at first.

I'd lowered my expectations considerably before arriving, knowing from seven other overseas postings (and another in my own country) that high expectations can be one's downfall. So as excited as I was, I'd also given myself a good talking to, and reminded myself about the traffic, the bureaucracy, the transportation hassles, the jet lag, the temporary apartment and the living out of suitcases. I figured, OK, if I keep my expectations low, there won't be any culture shock.

But what I hadn't prepared for was my attitude towards myself—the fact that I expected more from myself as a veteran of so many moves. If I were stuck in an African backwater or a former Soviet republic, I'd feel justified in some initial feelings of being overwhelmed and a bit lost.

But I'm in Rome, our dream post. The city in which we've always wanted to live.

Believe it or not, sometimes the glamour posts are the hardest to adjust to initially. Please don't scoff: I'm not complaining about being in Rome. But therein lies the problem: no matter what happens, I feel as if I simply *can't* complain about being in Rome. No one will take me seriously, least of all myself.

The thing is, Rome really *is* wonderful—I know that, and you know that. There's incredible pasta and fabulous ice cream and to-die-for coffee. Every church has a concert series; every garden has fountains and statues. One park near us, right in the center of the city, has a pond with dozens of turtles sunning themselves among the lily pads. Every time I take a walk, each turn yields new delights in this amazing place. Believe me, we are enjoying those things immensely, and we keep pinching ourselves to see when we're going to wake up.

And yet—I'm also trying to wake up from jet lag. Our temporary apartment had a huge leak and the bedroom carpet is soaked and mildewed, triggering allergies among the children. Every day I seem to do nothing but schlep things here, schlep things there: milk, boxes I'd mailed to myself, housewares and cleaning supplies, and still, there's always some essential we forgot to buy or just can't find. I've learned that some buses come early, some late and some not at all. When the latter occurs, I've had a devil of a time trying to find a taxi. I've dragged my children all over town, looking at maps and figuring out where to buy tickets. Depending on my mood (and my moods are quite changeable these days), it's either a terrific new adventure or it's a giant hassle.

In short, I'm starting all over again, just when I'd gotten the routine down in the last place. Every city, every country has its rhythm, and I've yet to mesh my own rhythm with Rome's. That doesn't have much to do with Rome, but a lot more to do with my place here, or lack thereof. I could be in Baku or Lagos and the reaction would likely be the same: I just don't belong here yet. I'm some strange thing out of context. I have not yet adapted.

Yes, it'll come. But how do I make it come faster?

Ironically, perhaps the most important way to help myself and my family through this time is not to rush things. Adjustment comes at its own speed; I can't make it arrive more quickly by forcing it. So I'm trying not to expect so much of myself—or my family. In fact, our daily reminder to ourselves is: slow down and do one thing at a time.

For this typical American, that's not an easy thing to do, but it's a necessary one. My tendency at normal times is to fill up the calendar, and I know I'm not alone. Most people these days schedule every hour of every day, whether it's with meetings, lunch dates, playdates, volunteer groups or running errands.

But when you're in a new country, it takes all your energy and time to do just one thing. One seemingly simple job such as finding a broom, or getting a document, can often turn into a half-day procedure when you don't know the ropes and barely know the language.

Not only that, but do I really want to spend every day doing just necessary things? We also need time for discovery and delight. A frustrating few hours trying to gather school supplies for the kids yielded a part of town where artists' galleries and craftsmen's shops abound. A walk in search of milk turned up not only milk, but also a Romanesque courtyard surrounding a fountain of spouting bronze frogs.

I'm learning, once again, that in the Strange Time of the Newly Arrived—an intense time in both good and bad ways—I simply need to go at a slower pace. So my calendar has one thing on it each day, and one thing only. And that's OK, even kind of wonderful, and liberating.

In fact, the Italians have a phrase for it: *piano a piano*. Step by step. One thing at a time.

Traveling with Pets

by Mette Beecroft

In the Foreign Service, we regularly look for ways to make a new post and a new house start to feel like "home." Family pets are often a very important aspect of this effort. In fact, our son used to say, "Home is where my cats are."

Traveling with pets has always necessitated careful planning—travel reservations, travel cases, food, water, litter boxes, litter and shots. However, travelers now must realize that the situation has become more complex, both because of airline restrictions and because of Department of State regulations. At the same time, foreign flag carriers still offer flexible service and acceptable solutions for arranging pet travel. There are also excellent sources of information. The important thing is to start early to make plans based on both travel options and on any possible restrictions at the post of assignment.

Several U.S. flag carriers have imposed embargoes on shipping pets between May and September, either as accompanied baggage or as cargo. This is the period when temperatures are apt to be highest (above 85F). However, in addition to the seasonal embargo, carriers may also refuse to transport pets in extreme temperatures at any time of year—above 85F or below 45F. And some breeds of pets, both dogs and cats that are "snub-nosed,"are even less able to tolerate extreme heat and cold because of a weak respiratory system. These temperature limits are set by the U.S. Department of Agriculture. In a requirement mostly driven by liability considerations, some airlines require pets to be shipped as cargo using a commercial pet shipper who then technically assumes responsibility.

As for regulations, and speaking generally, both the Fly America Act (which is based on law) and city-pair/contract fares reduce the possibilities for the State Department employee to transport household pets. The basic question often is: How do I send my pet when the airline I am supposed to use—because of Fly America or contract fare limitations—has an embargo on pets?

It is important to remember that pets are not obliged to travel with the employee and are not bound by Fly America or contract fare considerations. Thus, they can be sent via airline cargo service or via a licensed commercial pet shipper on any carrier, U.S. or foreign, which will accept them. If a commercial pet shipper is not used, the employee has the opportunity to design a route that is in the interest of the pet (e.g. few layovers or travel at night) and to investigate travel conditions (e.g. cabin temperature and pressure). Most airlines have a mechanism for providing food and water for live cargo. And the airfare for shipping an animal (not the shipper's handling charges) is reimbursable under the Miscellaneous Portion of the Foreign Transfer Allowance (Standardized Regulations 240) or under the Miscellaneous Portion of the Home Transfer Allowance (Standardized Regulations 250). If total reimbursement is not available through one of the two Transfer Allowances, charges for shipping an animal may be listed as a moving expense for income tax purposes.

At least in theory, there are four ways for a cat or dog to travel via the airlines, but not every airline has all four options available. Ultimately, most pets will probably not travel on U.S. flag carriers because foreign flag carriers offer more flexibility.

1. Sometimes, the pet is permitted to travel on the plane with the traveler in the cabin but usually not more than one or two animals per flight. The animal must be small enough to fit under the seat in a carrier. There is usually no extra charge for bringing a small animal in the cabin.

2. A pet can also travel as accompanied baggage. The animal travels on the same plane as its owner but in the baggage compartment of the plane. The pet owner should ascertain that the space where the animal will travel is temperature controlled and pressurized. When the pet travels as accompanied baggage, transportation costs are charged accordingly. This method is the most economical of the cargo options.

3. The pet can be booked on a separate flight as cargo on any airline that will accept it, including foreign flag carriers. The rate is considerably more than for accompanied baggage, but the pet owner gains travel options for the pet that need not comply with Fly America or contract fare stipulations.

4. The pet can be shipped through a licensed commercial shipper who specializes in the shipment of pets and other live animals. For pet owners, this method is the most "hassle-free," in that the pet shipper picks up the animal and it is delivered at destination. The shipper also takes care of documentation and will arrange for care and feeding along the way. This method is also the most expensive.

Because U.S. airline policies on pet travel change frequently, it is not practical to summarize them. The Overseas Briefing Center (OBC) maintains a website which contains valuable information and resource links on pet travel. The INTRANET address is: **http://fsi-web.fsi.state.gov/fsi/tc/obc/pets/default.asp** For specific questions, contact the Overseas Briefing Center at (703) 302 7277. Additional information is also contained in State ALDAC (to all diplomatic and consular posts) cable 072825, dated April, 2002.

Even though arranging pet travel can be a complicating factor, if the pet is a well-established member of the family, it is important to make every effort to bring it along if at all possible. Our son was absolutely serious when he said, "Home is where my cats are." And I must admit, his parents felt the same way.

PART III
Views from Abroad

Letters from Ethiopia

by Karen DeThomas

June 1990

Dear Folks,

We've passed the medical exams with flying colors, gotten our hepatitis B, yellow fever and typhoid shots and have officially received orders for a three-year tour in Addis Ababa, Ethiopia. I am a bit unnerved by this one. It is so far and remote and poor. But I've always been a good soldier and will tough it out.

Soon packing boxes will appear and our dishes, books, pictures, toys and bicycles will be whisked away. We won't have a large shipment since our furniture will be put into storage. The house in Addis will be furnished with "representational" furniture since part of our job will be entertaining.

This will be my seventh packout in 13 years. At this point merely the sight of packing material and boxes brings on hyperventilation—but it does give me the opportunity to give the back of the refrigerator a good cleaning.

Joe really wants to be a Deputy Chief of Mission so he can, as he says, "show the Department what I can do." It is posts like Addis that allow a relatively young officer to have the opportunity to be the Number Two. I will watch over Ben and Gaby and fight to keep them well and safe. I will also be a "wife-of" but certainly not from the old school where high-ranking wives strong-armed the wives of subordinates into passing cookies around at teas. We are all in this together to try and make the Embassy community a viable entity for our children while furthering the interests of the U.S. abroad. So there.

June 1990

Dear Folks,

It was really hard for me to say goodbye too. I promise I will work very hard to keep your grandchildren safe and well. Going to Ethiopia is my gift to Joe. I will write when I get there.

July 1990

Helloe frome Merrye Olde Englande,

After an overnight flight we arrived at our hotel mid-morning. Being too tried and grimy for sightseeing, we sat in the lobby waiting for our room to be ready. Overcome by jetlag, I promptly fell asleep. Apparently the sight of a snoozing traveler surrounded with 10 pieces of non-matching luggage was too much for the management—the Desk Clerk was able, quite unexpectedly, to find us a room.

The next day Joe had some business to conduct at the Embassy, so I took the children on a mini-tour of London—a city I am particularly partial to. Never take your children to a place close to your heart because they will look at it with different eyes and cause you to question your taste. Gaby found London dirty and noisy. She was not impressed with Westminster, Waterloo Bridge or Buckingham Palace and was only mildly moved by the Changing of the Horse Guards. Ben was hungry and on the prowl for a McDonald's. Maybe when they are older…

July 1990

Dear Folks,

The flight to Addis was long. We left London at 11 p.m. and arrived here early the next morning, crossing several time zones. I do find it off-putting to meet people I wish to make a good first impression upon while wearing the clothes I slept in. But meet them I did. The Chargé met us in his official car—a large white Cadillac. He is a lovely man who inspires calm and confidence.

Soon we were on our way to what would be our new home—whisked away in his car with the small American flags attached to the hood blowing crisply in the breeze. I must say we made people sit up and take notice.

I took notice too. The streets are lined with corrugated tin and mud huts, which serve as housing for the majority of Addis citizens. Cows, donkeys, sheep and goats compete for the roadway.

My first impression was of poverty on a vast scale, but what did I expect? In Mexico and Iran poverty was in pockets. Here it is in your face everywhere. I really had to try to keep the lump in my throat from being accompanied by tears.

After a 15-minute drive we arrived at the Embassy compound. It is quite lovely. A profusion of flowers surround the chancery. There are fourteen housing units—houses and duplexes and the Marine House.

We were led into our rather grand home and introduced to our staff. Mamo, our houseman, is 75 if he is a day and with his slight build and shaved head he reminds me of Gandhi. Our cook, Truwerk ("True work") is about my age. She does not speak English, but having worked for the Cuban Embassy she can speak Spanish—so that is the language we will discuss menus in. Atsede, our very sweet cleaning person, has taken a shine to Ben.

Our house is a large stone rambler with a huge living room (for entertaining), a large dining room (for entertaining) and a vast kitchen (for cooking the food with which to entertain). This area is the public area. Three bedrooms, a den and three baths make up the family quarters. A glass enclosed sun porch overlooks an Eden-like garden alive with blue hydrangea. This joint is a residence; mind you, not a mere house.

The compound is surrounded by a six-foot stone wall. With Ethiopian guards patrolling its perimeter, it is remarkably safe and reminds me of a small town in the fifties. Gaby has met two little girls who live just down the street and they are becoming great friends. If Gaby is happy her mama is happy.

One of my first projects is to hire a nanny for Gaby and Ben since I am expected to attend and hostess cocktail parties, dinner parties, visiting dignitary parties, national day parties, hello parties and goodbye parties to the tune of two to three a week. I am limiting these "representational events" to two a week. Italy will not suffer if I don't show up at its national day, but my children might suffer if they don't know how much I care.

September 1990

Dear Folks,

We took an official trip to meet the elders of the ancient town of Ankobar and view the old church that is of great historical significance as the site of several royal coronations over the centuries. Joe and I accompanied the Chargé and his very nice wife along with the Public Affairs officer and a visiting historian. Gaby and Ben sensibly stayed at home with Nanny Fikarte and several Disney movies.

The first two hours passed uneventfully on a paved two-lane road. From Addis we left the highlands and made our way to the warmer lowlands. While it isn't necessary to take malarial suppressants on the high plateau, any trip into the lowlands requires a month long regime of the foul stuff. Since malaria is a potentially fatal disease, there is no kidding around with it.

The countryside is dotted with homesteads comprised of a *tukul*—a round building made of mud with a thatched roof—surrounded with a fence made of tree branches. Cattle are highly prized and surprisingly are taken care of by children—who are entrusted with the responsibility of the family's source of wealth. Fields are planted with *tef*—grain used to make *injera*, the flat sour pancake which is the staff of life in Ethiopia.

The last hours of travel were slow on a gravel and dirt road where few vehicles have gone before. We finally arrived at Ankobar, dusty but game, to be met by the village elders and taken for a tour of the church in use today—complete with *Tabot* (Bible) and ceremonial crowns proudly laid out for our inspection.

Christianity made its way to Ethiopia in the 4th or 5th century and its ceremonies remain closer to the early days of Christianity than in the west. Religion is a great solace to Ethiopians and helps them get through situations horrific enough to stop even the strongest in their tracks. How I admire them.

Finally the elders pointed to a steep hill, bordered on one side by a nasty ravine and invited us to climb to the top to view the ruins of the old church. We began our ascent by winding around the side with the nasty ravine.

Remembering that these people would form lasting impressions of Americans by my conduct I smiled bravely and tried—really. But heights next to bottomless pits into which I might fall simply do me in. I envisioned making one misstep and plunging into the yawning abyss. Besides, I gave birth to two children without drugs of any kind and once had three teeth filled without Novocaine, so what did I have to prove?

With all the dignity I could muster I returned to the foot of the mountain, gently refusing our hosts' gallant offer to carry me up to the clouds. It was really quite pleasant sitting on the fallen tree trunk and sharing my box of vanilla wafers with some children who gathered around me.

After an hour of pastoral bliss my companions returned. But the day was not over. The villagers announced they were making a feast in our honor and to prove it, led a tethered lamb toward us. Apparently the woolly thing was to be the entrée. We all strenuously shook our heads, thanked the villagers for their thoughtfulness and pled for Lamb Chop's life. Interpreting our pleas for politeness, they did the poor lamb in.

When the food was ready we were led into a small shed where a long plank served as a table. Dinner consisted of injera, a meat dish (need I say more?) and some homemade *talla*—a fermented honey drink that has the ability to make one very silly real quick.

I'd never been on so intimate acquaintance with the main course before. I managed to daintily nibble a bit in addition to stuffing some in my purse when nobody was looking.

However, I am not unmindful that it was a great honor to be feasted in such a manner by people who only eat meat on rare occasions.

P.S. I came home to find Ben and Mamo reenacting a sword fight between a musketeer (Ben) and a minion of Cardinal Richelieu (Mamo) with the minion getting the worst of it.

December 1990

Dear Folks,

I was among a group of Embassy wives who recently traveled to southern Ethiopia to tour the Swedish Burn Hospital of Ethiopia. In the traditional *tukul*, cooking fires are set on the floor in the middle of the main room. Children playing nearby are often easy prey.

It took us nearly all day to reach the hospital. The landscape is wonderful—off the highlands the land becomes lusher until it turns tropical with flowers in wonderful colors and a gorgeous array of birds.

A tour of the wards gave us ample opportunity to witness the utter misery that man's most basic tool can do. The hospital staff is very capable and does an excellent job but it seems that burns are the most painful of injuries and require a long and difficult convalescence. Apparently even after one recuperates from the horror, they are often so physically scarred they are unable to return to society.

The tour concluded with a 6-month old with several burns covering a large part of her body. She had somehow rolled into the cooking fire. Even though she was receiving excellent care, she was not given a good chance of survival. A beautiful pair of eyes stared out of a horribly damaged body. I am surprised I didn't start sobbing aloud. I never want to see such anguish again. I wanted to run and not stop until I never had to witness children hungry and injured again. Is there such a paradise?

Ironically there is—and I found it at the end of my journey. A flower-filled house where two exuberant, nearly perfect children ran to greet me. I am at odds about what I can do in the face of this overwhelming poverty I face every time I leave my compound. What is needed? Money, time, patronage? I must try to find what I should do if I am going to survive this.

Happily, this time I could do something. The hospital desperately needs a skin graft machine to allow larger amounts of skin to be grafted and hasten the recovery process. A few of us got together and hosted a musical evening and supper to foot the bill for a skin graft machine that should be making its way to Addis as we speak.

January 1991

Dear Folks,

Hello from the Nile; I am in Egypt! Fourteen of us from the international community led by the wife of the Egyptian ambassador will spend 9 days here. I was born wanting to go to Egypt! I've never left my children for that long but Joe assures me that he, along with a houseman, nanny, cook, maid and gardener should be able to keep track of a nine-year old and a three-year old.

My fellow travelers are a delight. We are very international and come from Turkey, Sweden, China, the UK, Peru and Indonesia. I feel like a kid on a school holiday.

We spent today at the pyramids. Last night we floated down the Nile on a barge complete with dinner and dancing—done mainly by a belly dancer. I hate it when performers coax poor unwitting tourists to join them on stage and try to do dances that often take years of study.

The only reason I agreed to er…dance was because every other table had offered up a victim. Besides, I saw the video that the Turkish Ambassador took and I think, all in all, my performances could be described as rather tasteful.

November 1991

Dear Folks,

The Embassy hosted an Election Party at the ballroom of the Hilton Hotel—the closest thing to a modern hotel in all Ethiopia.

A large television screen was set up against the back wall with six or seven smaller sets scattered through the ballroom showing live network coverage and excerpts from the campaign from a satellite feed.

It was a smashing success. Well over 400 people from the diplomatic and Ethiopian community as well as relief agencies spent the entire night watching the returns.

When President Bush made his concession speech, many Ethiopians (with memories of the violent civil war so fresh) marveled that he handed over power in a peaceful manner and even offered to help Clinton during the transition. We demonstrated to all how our system of government works. I was very proud to be an American.

January 1992

Dear Folks,

Joe and I went off in search of the source of the Blue Nile this week. Lake Tana is not only one of the sources of the Nile but is also regarded as a very holy place by the devout. Many small churches dot its shore. The lake ends abruptly as the water plunges hundreds of feet to become the Blue Nile, which then meanders to Khartoum to meet the White Nile, which becomes the NILE (that is enough geography for today). The falls is breathtaking—certainly a competitor for Niagara.

On the way back to the Land Rover we met a ten-year-old child-bride. She was married but not living with her husband yet—she would go to him at maturity. She was Gaby's age and behaved like the little girl she was. I wanted to smuggle her home to play Barbies with Gabs.

September 1992

Dear Folks,

A good friend and I have taken on a project at a school/orphanage on the outskirts of town. Children reside at the orphanage and attend school there until 8th grade. Then, in order to attend high school each child must pass a "school-leaving" test. The kicker is that the test and the language of high school and university is English—an unusual choice considering that the longtime Marxist government really didn't care for English speakers.

We will conduct an English lesson to 7th and 8th grade for 2 hours every Thursday. The kids leap to their feet when we enter the classroom and hang onto our every utterance—you can bet that the pearls of wisdom originating from my mouth are not especially noteworthy, but education is greatly respected in Ethiopia.

Between classes we retire to the Teachers' Room and drink very strong, very sweet tea. We talk politics with the teachers who make approximately $200 a year.

May 1993

Dear Folks,

We are coming home in July. Gaby will begin middle school and Ben will start kindergarten in their own country. I want them to always know they are Americans. But I sincerely hope when I am driving around Arlington, Virginia to the orthodontist or the grocery store that I will remember what I have seen here and that it not recede into a hazy half-forgotten dream but continue prompting me to remember and react.

Love,
Karen

A Day in the Life of a Foreign Service Family in Beijing

by Fritz Galt

It's Sunday morning. We perform our exercise bicycle routine in our high-rise apartment, and watch a blue sky dawn over the city. Eat breakfast of *dou jiang*, a tofu drink costing only 2 cents from the local grocery, and apple turnovers that cost a dollar apiece from the local Vie de France.

For our weekly sightseeing, we make a quick decision to taxi to Jing-shan, a mountain built from the excavated dirt of the moat around the Forbidden City.

We walk through a park that is teeming with Chinese on their day off. Three singing groups have formed under the trees and are singing their hearts out. Whether for art or exercise, it's hard to tell. An accordion and a single-stringed bowed instrument called an *er-hu* accompany them.

Up the steep mountain, we encounter two forms of wildlife, a bird and a chipmunk, two rarities in the middle of this giant, paved city. We see a man walk down the steep hill through the trees with a saxophone around his neck.

We reach the summit where there is a huge, square pagoda with views over the immense Forbidden City and the lakes just to the west, including Chungnan Hai where the party leaders live in seclusion, and Bei Hai, which is open as a park.

My wife receives a cellphone call just as I'm lining my family up precariously for a picture, and we spend the next fifteen minutes impatiently listening to her discuss the next day's Treasury Secretary's visit.

We eat peanut butter and jelly sandwiches under the shade of the next pagoda down the hill, and watch streams of French and Chinese tourists climb up and down the hill. A team of gray-uniformed soldiers and medics in crisp white uniforms carry an empty stretcher, a gurney, and medical bags back down the hill from some emergency at the summit.

A local lady thrusts her daughter at my children to take their picture together. We don't resist too hard, and a crowd of thirty interested faces watches the picture being taken.

At the bottom of the hill, we observe the spot where the last Ming Emperor hanged himself after killing his family, rather than facing a peasant uprising.

We taxi home just in time for my daughter to go to a friend's birthday party one floor below ours. It's another PartyExpress.com special.

My wife, son, and I sneak out of the building for a quick shopping run. In our underground parking lot, we have to figure out which dust-coated car is ours. It has lost its red sheen over the course of the week due to building construction and a dry countryside.

Our garage exit is closed due to one more "repair," so it takes us a while to find another exit out of the complex.

Our normal black-market car wash shop has been demolished, so we use a "legal" looking one, that washes and dries by hand for a reasonable 25 cents.

The local government-run Friendship Store for imported items is under reconstruction, but still open for "businese." There we can buy most anything, at a price. But who would pay $8.00 for a pack of Rice Krispies Snacks? Other things are within our price range, with a variety of product brands available, mostly from Europe. Last year's Christmas tinsel still hanging over the cashiers does make you wonder if the food is also out of date.

Shady trees line the streets of the diplomatic neighborhood adjoining our high-rise complex. People casually pedal bicycles everywhere.

For over a year, local residents protesting the use of the alley beside their apartment building have periodically blocked one convenient entrance to our complex. Often it is littered with broken bottles and old people sitting in the road, so we don't even try that access. But, we also expect our normal car entrance to be blocked for repairs, so we try another entrance, only to find that one closed, and our original one open.

We cart groceries upstairs. On my way back down the elevator to return the cart, another couple enters several floors below me. I think I should know who they are, since they look like they're from the Embassy, but I don't, and it's an awkward ride down. Where's Muzak when you need it? Such a big Embassy, and a big turnover each year.

We relax at home with books and ironing, and we try to watch the remainder of *Citizen Kane*, a movie we started watching a year ago, and have only had a free minute or two to watch once every month or so since then. We don't get a chance to finish it before the kids wake from their naps.

We cook a dinner of chicken from the commissary, vegetables from the local grocery, and Rice-a-Roni from a recently opened private import store. It goes down well with *Les Miserables* playing on CD and a candlelit table.

We're all a little sick these days, with a cold and a urinary tract infection, and mild stomach upset. My wife may have pinpointed the upset down to a rancid-smelling tub of margarine. Sure enough, our son wakes up repeatedly sick that night.

Life here has its amusements, and its obstacles. Some days one wins over the other. Today, both sides win.

Highlights from 26 Years in the Foreign Service

by Debbi Miller

In Barbados I "had" a large troop of wild golden monkeys who came to my courtyard every evening to partake of the fruit of an indigenous apple tree, and they became fond of me, and responsive to me, as a result of my daily appearance with bunches of bananas. Some of them were brave enough to come quite close to me, and after a time two of them actually sat on my lap to eat. I watched over the months as they became pregnant, and as their babies grew and developed unique personalities and faces, and as they shunned a maimed member of the troop, etc., etc., etc.—and it was magical and bewitching and haunting and could never have happened in the United States.

Back when Yugoslavia was still called Yugoslavia, I visited the crystal works in Rogaska, and came away with some exquisite vases, jars and bowls for literally pennies…and besides being beautiful they are now exceedingly rare and valuable.

I organized, publicized, and sang a benefit concert for the New Zealand Women's Refuge (domestic violence is a real issue in New Zealand), and had the deep satisfaction of seeing my financial contribution put to work. Later I sang another concert to benefit Save The Children, an international organization. Nothing can compare to the joy and fulfillment of doing what I love most and seeing it mean something positive in the world. I didn't sock away big bucks for my retirement, nor did I beef up my resume…but I engaged my passion unforgettably.

I'm a stay-at-home mom who has been, from time to time, liberated from the drudgery of housekeeping by the affordable maids overseas, and not only has my own life been more enjoyable for that, but my children have had a happier, more relaxed, more creative mom who has had plenty of time for them. No one can measure the value of that.

My list could go on for hours, but you get the idea…this life is stress-filled, danger-filled, challenge-filled, requiring flexibility and adaptive skills "out the wazoo"—but it is also rich and surprising and satisfying and inspiring and humbling and fun! You must be realistic about what the restrictions and difficulties are, and what you think you can bear, and what you cannot. But fear not! Adventure awaits!

Pining for Pop-Tarts: One Family's Foreign Service Food Experiences

by Patricia Linderman

As my husband and I were getting ready for our first post, Port of Spain, we were asked if we would be shipping "consumables." Evidently, the supermarket situation in Trinidad was considered deficient by American standards at that time, so the government would pay to ship canned foods, laundry detergent and similar items to post for us.

What a wimpy idea, I thought. The people in Trinidad must have some kind of food to eat. And they wash their clothes somehow, don't they? We'll just do as they do—and really get an inside view of a new culture, part of the reason we entered Foreign Service life in the first place.

One of my first outings in Trinidad was to a bookstore, where I bought a local cookbook, a small, orange paperback called "Our Cooking." And during the next few days, while my husband started work behind a visa window at the Embassy, I wandered through stores trying to match products to recipes.

To save time, I decided to eliminate any dishes that involved hammering, grating, liquefying and straining fresh coconuts. I also crossed off foo-foo, a cornmeal dish that had to be stirred "for several hours until thick." And while "buss-up-shut"—shredded flatbread to accompany curry—sounded good, I didn't have a clue how to "pound" it, and we had no "hot griddle stone" in our temporary apartment.

In the supermarket itself, I was amazed to find that an entire aisle was taken up by different kinds of canned peas. The "beef" cooler contained no recognizable steaks or hamburger, just dark frozen lumps labeled "oxtail."

At least I recognized a few things. Eggs are rather unmistakable. I found milk and orange juice in longlife boxes. Instant coffee. Sugar. And something approximating the ingredients of ham sandwiches. So we survived the days that followed. And every one brought new discoveries: the sweetest pineapples we'd ever eaten; fresh papaya; and tiny finger bananas with more flavor in each one than a whole Chiquita.

Simple snack bars in town sold delicious curried chicken, potato or goat (actually, I can't tell you whether the goat was delicious) wrapped up in a pancake called "roti." At the beach, enterprising vendors fried shark fillets and puffy balls of dough in vats of oil to make "shark and bake" sandwiches topped with a lime and cilantro sauce. Men with shiny machetes (picturesquely called "cutlasses") would neatly lop an end off a green coconut and offer it with a straw as a refreshing drink.

We were surprised at first by what the local stores didn't have. No berries of any kind, or broccoli—they are cool-weather crops. Apples were an expensive, imported delicacy. There were no convenience foods, nothing "low-fat" or "sugar-free." No Mexican food—until someone met an enterprising Venezuelan lady who made tortilla chips in her kitchen, and from then on she took orders and made weekly deliveries to the Embassy. Someone else did the same for bagels. (And if cream cheese to go with them appeared at one of the local shops, the news was announced in the Embassy newsletter!)

There was one little "international gourmet" shop in a mall, where you could get things like dusty boxes of macaroni and cheese mix, or small jars of peanut butter, for about four dollars. Sometimes we did, out of homesickness more than hunger. We were surprised in general to find prices for food and household products generally high—local fruits and vegetables were inexpensive, but manufactured goods and imports were more expensive than in the States.

So our friends who had shipped consumables often saved money, but they faced their own problems. One couple found that their cereal and crackers had been packed together with cleaning products, picking up just enough of a soapy taste to make them inedible. And of course there was no way to ship broccoli in consumables, or fresh steak and hamburger (actually, the military representatives at post were able to bring in some beef on a supply flight, to widespread envy).

I never learned to make the recipes in "Our Cooking," and most of the cookbooks I'd brought from home were useless—there was always at least one unavailable ingredient in each recipe (like "one 10 ½ ounce can of cream of mushroom soup"—forget it). But the American Women's Club self-published a very helpful cookbook with recipes adapted to local conditions, including the necessary measurements and substitutions.

At our second post, Santiago, Chile, there was a small commissary on the Embassy grounds. It reminded me of a convenience store, although with even higher prices, and some items past their expiration dates due to long shipping times. However, we appreciated the American foods, especially since we now had a young son who loved things like American cereals, macaroni and cheese, and brown sugar cinnamon Pop-Tarts.

One complication of our eating habits in Chile was the need to disinfect fruits and vegetables. The irrigation water for many farms evidently ran through villages without sewer systems. So everything had to be either cooked, peeled or soaked in the sink with a disinfectant solution (we used a local product called Zonalin, but diluted bleach also works). And we were advised not to eat certain hard-to-clean items, like lettuce and strawberries, at all.

Life without lettuce was strange at first, but we learned that Chileans add a layer of sliced or pureed avocado to their sandwiches instead (yum), and a typical salad was made from peeled tomatoes, sliced onions and lime juice (it's still one of my favorites).

And again there were wonderful new foods to discover, like chiri-moya fruit (cut up and served in a bowl with fresh orange juice) and empanadas baked in a wood-fired oven. The salmon and beef were especially good, and outstanding wines of all varieties were only a few dollars a bottle. Unfortunately, however, the chicken always had an off-putting fishy taste—the birds were fed fishmeal, which Chile pro-duces in abundant supply.

Our third post was Havana, Cuba, in its fifth year of food crisis after the collapse of the Soviet Union. As privileged foreigners, we were able to shop at the *Diplosupermercado*, a grocery store where customers had to pay (ironically enough) in U.S. dollars rather than Cuban pesos. Even so, the place was dark, smelled bad, and offered a wildly fluctuat-ing selection of products. There might be no butter or eggs for weeks. If you wanted cheese, for instance, the only choice might be a big block, of one kind only, at an outrageous price. Bread came in square or rounded loaves, but only one flavor: sawdust. Some American prod-ucts were regularly re-exported from Mexico after their expiration dates—we'd see Halloween-themed cereal boxes in March, and we learned that diet sodas taste even more horrible after the date stamped on the bottom of the can.

Fortunately, we had wised up about consumables this time around. We shipped things like flour and other baking ingredients, canned goods, cleaning products, and a well-guarded supply of treats. The Interests Section (as our pseudo-Embassy was called) issued us two large refrigerators and an upright freezer in our housing, so we could buy and hoard scarce foods in season or when they appeared in the store.

With the help of our hoarded goods and consumables, we learned to cook most of our favorite foods from scratch—pizza dough with the help of a bread machine, tomato sauce from fresh tomatoes in season and frozen in ziplock bags, yogurt from a countertop yogurt maker. We called it "Homesteading in Havana." I even learned how to make pita bread at home—did you know that it puffs up in the oven and then collapses to form the pocket?

And meanwhile, even in Havana we found new foods we loved. Fried plantains, both green and ripe. Rice and black beans, of course, cooked all day with lots of seasoning (after a good washing and careful removal of little stones and other debris). And the fruit—we had a tiny yard, but it contained a grapefruit tree, coconut palm, avocado tree, lime tree and several banana plants (unfortunately, the way it worked was that a huge stalk of bananas would grow slowly and then ripen all at once, so we had no bananas for weeks, and suddenly hundreds of bananas to share with friends for a few quick days until they turned black!). By this time, we had two young sons, and they still remember Havana as a time of good homemade food and togetherness in the kitchen.

Our fourth post, Leipzig, Germany, was clearly a food paradise compared to Cuba. We reveled in German whole-wheat breads, creamy yogurt and *Streuselkuchen* (crumb cake) with all sorts of fresh berries (finally, berries!). If we weren't satisfied yet, we could drive three hours to a U.S. military base to stock up on the uniquely American foods not stocked by German stores, such as cranberry sauce, turkey stuffing, brownie mix, Bisquick, Oreos, Trix, pecans, chocolate chips, cornbread mix, refried beans, Ranch salad dressing—and of course those brown sugar cinnamon Pop-Tarts. (Where we could really have used a military commissary was in Cuba, but Guantanamo Bay was separated from us by barbed wire and minefields, not to mention hundreds of miles!). To further spoil us, we could even order non-perishable groceries by Internet direct from the United States.

I thought we had access to nearly every conceivable food, but then we returned to Washington after twelve years abroad and wandered around the 24-hour Giant in a state of culinary culture shock. Pesto hummus? Lobster ravioli? Frozen organic Indian meals? I know this stuff wasn't here when we left. The range of international foods available seems to have exploded (great for us Foreign Service types), but it also seems that Americans expect a huge and growing range of products on their store shelves (not so great for those of you going out into the less-well-stocked world).

In the Foreign Service, you're not likely to find gourmet foods from dozens of nations (only from the nation you happen to be in, and maybe a neighbor or two). You probably won't find frozen convenience foods, chili-lime tortilla chips, or your favorite brand of cracker (our favorite gifts from visiting friends and relatives abroad were boxes of Stoned Wheat Thins).

But you may have a cook or a housekeeper making you a delicious local dinner, and maybe even doing your shopping. You may have fishermen coming to your garden gate to sell you their fresh catch. You will most probably be invited by local people to share their cuisine—an unforgettable experience, whether you end up liking the food or not. And when all else fails, at most posts you can at least order brown sugar cinnamon Pop-Tarts from NetGrocer!

Shopping as a Cross-Cultural Experience

by Melissa Brayer Hess

Most people find food shopping routine and unexciting. However, as a Foreign Service spouse who has lived and shopped in different cultures, I have found shopping anything but dull. Whether in Paris arguing with an irritated fruit vendor, in Kaduna bargaining with a Nigerian merchant, or in Leningrad waiting in line with Russian babushkas, I view buying food as an opportunity to learn about people.

Parisian markets were bountifully supplied with beautifully-displayed fruits and vegetables. Despite the enticing surroundings, impatient Parisian merchants often made shopping an unpleasant experience. Merchants shouted at me for selecting my own fruit, instead of asking for assistance from the clerk, scolded me for requesting vegetables by the piece, rather than by the kilo, and chided me for having the temerity to give back items I considered to be of unacceptable quality. Shopkeepers even snubbed me for making grammatical errors in French. They preferred no business at all to dealing with requests that disrupted their accustomed patterns.

In Nigeria, foreigners were always struck by the shocking physical features and pervasive smells of the Kaduna Central Market. Meat and produce lay unrefrigerated all day under a hot African sun. Unbathed humans and animals lounged in every shady corner. People urinated wherever they found a spot. By the end of the day, the combination of smells could overpower the foreign shopper. The profusion of physically deformed beggars also shocked foreign visitors. Blind people sang for alms, and polio victims crawled about dragging their bent, withered legs through the dust. Even lepers with faces and fingers eaten away by the disease approached shoppers for money.

Despite the disease and poverty, however, shopping at the Kaduna market was usually a pleasant experience, because whether the merchant's approach was relaxed or aggressive, he always treated the customer in a human way. Even hard bargaining sessions ended with a laugh and a smile. My limited use of Hausa, the local language, occasioned amazement and pleasure—far different from the disdainful looks produced by my language deficiencies in French markets. One merchant regularly gave me a few extra tomatoes—what the Nigerians call "a dash"—to encourage my continued patronage. The merchants' livelihood depended on shoppers. Their interaction with customers, far from being a nuisance, represented for them an essential and valued part of their profession.

Shoppers, not merchants, fill my marketplace memories of Leningrad. Russians took shopping seriously. Basic foods were available, but if the homemaker wanted more than cabbage and beets, she had to constantly be alert for the unexpected discovery. A centrally-planned economy grew and distributed food according to the dictates of the bureaucracy, not the consumer. In theory, this provided for a "scientific" distribution of food among the populace, but no Soviet citizen was ever able to unravel the logic of the system. No one knew when or where bananas would next appear. Vegetable stalls would be flooded with oranges one week—the next week oranges would disappear completely. The shopper's creed was "Be prepared." No woman would venture out without her "just-in-case" carrying sack and roll of rubles. If a line began to form, the astute shopper joined in first and asked questions later. While line "standees "often seemed gruff and "pushy" to me, line-standing had its own code of etiquette, and any breach of the rules brought instant admonishments from one's fellow citizens. No one cut into line except the handicapped, veterans with proper

I.D., and occasionally women carrying babies. It was acceptable, however, to ask the person in front of you to hold your place while you went to do other shopping. In fact, the seasoned shopper would work two or three lines simultaneously.

Food shopping in a foreign culture gives an outsider the opportunity to observe the "natives" in one of their most fundamental, unadorned activities. Shopping is an excellent way to see how people interact with one another and offers clues to basic values. In every Foreign Service post, there is much that can be learned about people by interacting with them in ordinary, daily activities. The opportunities abound, if we are attentive and look for them.

*This essay first appeared in the "Tips from the Trenches" section of Foreign Service Lifelines, at **www.aafsw.org**.*

In the Eye of the Beholder

by Ann Bushnell

The ship moved gracefully away from New York as John and I turned from our final farewell waves. Our sudden outburst of spontaneous laughter and hugs conveyed a wordless paragraph of the wisdom of a delayed honeymoon. The three months since the wedding had been both exciting and busy as we prepared for our move to Bogota, where John's new assignment in the Foreign Service would allow a refreshing break from the Washington bureaucracy.

And what a honeymoon! Of the 100 passengers on the graceful liner, we were honored to be seated at the Captain's table, and other countless privileges surrounded us. As I sank into the large puffed feather cushion of the deck chair, I felt like I was in the pristine heavens that I saw looking down on me. Only after I returned to our cabin and opened the door to the fragrance of the newly-placed fresh towels did I know it. And heated water in the beautiful swimming pool—what an unexpected treat! I had to stop and remind myself from time to time that life in Bogota would be a far cry from this. Pampered, content, and in love with being in love, we succumbed to the luxury and romance that enveloped us. Evening breezes on the deck became less like November as we sailed blissfully toward the tropics.

Our dining table was highlighted by a most interesting couple who were officials of the Panama Canal, a Swedish Baron in search of some other identity, and a Chicago bank president who had just retired to breed strawberries on his extensive farm in Ohio, along with his new wife. The menus were a never-ending gastronomical experience worthy of the strictest food critics, with impeccable service and presentation. I could have thought I was in Buckingham Palace when the waiter expertly placed the miniature pastel mint figurines surrounding the perfectly timed raspberry souffle beside the finger bowl!

The Captain was a good storyteller and loved to recount his long years of experience at sea since his boyhood days in Norway. It was easy to detect an abbreviated version here and there in the presence of ladies. Our tablemate's knowledge of the canal operation was invaluable as he briefed us during the daylong passage through the locks. If I hadn't heard it from him, I would never have believed that the QE 2 would have only one inch of space on each side when going through, and was actually designed to canal measurements. Everything was just too good to be true, more than I could have asked for.

The Captain hurried away to his post at the bridge as we saw Buenaventura ahead, where we would be getting off. His last words before dutifully steering us to port had a casual urgency about them that puzzled me. John dismissed them with an air of ambivalent gratitude as he shook his head, saying we would be fine having dinner in town.

At first, the stifling air on deck went mostly unnoticed as I was intensely viewing the growing images of the Port approaching me, with rounded eyes, in every direction. As we got closer, the heat and humidity from land seemed to almost solidify the alien, grey air. I recognized the bold contrast to the luxury of our airconditioned ship with deck breezes. But never mind, I thought, this will last just the one night as we travel up the mountains tomorrow to Bogota.

Upon leaving the pier, I shuddered as I sensed that the scene before me was unreal; perhaps something removable at the director's signal. And then, my mind appeared and followed my eyes to a wavy blur, needing focus, of the big black birds with large beaks on the treetops, patiently watching the bony animals on the dusty and neglected ground below. Small stucco buildings hid the mud shacks and the barefoot children with swollen bellies from the sea. One wide avenue, of vintage pavement and suggesting onetime grandeur, drew the action from the port inland, past the scattered, crudely-made wooden vending carts strewn along the walls of faded mosaic patterns and mold that lined the avenue. Well, this heat is stifling all right, I thought, feeling myself shaken back to a burdened reality.

An old and tired taxi reluctantly managed us and our suitcases as the solicitous driver smiled and nodded optimistically as if to assure us that despite the several pairs of rosary beads hanging from the rear view mirror and knife tears in the upholstery, we would arrive momentarily at the Hotel Estacion. As my foggy mind caught up with my location, I realized that the missing windows were an extremely inadequate version of this taxi's air conditioning.

The hotel appeared weary and sad. A broken neon sign hung above the stucco porch; the two lone weathered and splintered rocking chairs were quietly abandoned to humming varieties of native insects. I took a curious peek around the veranda which stopped me suddenly—what might be a swimming pool of blue and white broken tiles, somehow still glossy, surrounded hundreds of patches of black scum. Something moved. Sure enough, there was water under the scum! After checking in to our selection that I had been assured was the best and the only hotel with a star in town, I found myself tightly clutching a bottle of soda water I somehow must have remembered to buy from the man we found, finally, resting beneath a rusty and noisy fan that bothered not even the emaciated cat dozing on the broken tile floor at his feet. Graham Greene would have been known to leave Borneo for this!

By now, everything we thought or did was followed limply by our blurred, sweaty bodies, as if we were programmed. We silently groaned at the two cots that barely hid their lumpy mattresses under a single muslin sheet. As my head managed to turn, I noticed the private bath we were promised; there sat a bare, yellowed toilet bowl that boasted its comfort with no seat, proudly visible through the doorless bath entrance.

It was then that John told me that the Captain had invited us back to dine, and we were gratefully back on the ship in no time, as he smiled at us knowingly. It didn't take me long to figure out that our steward on board would gladly find us a cabin to shower in, if not our own, and damned if I wouldn't bring the soap back to town with me. Suddenly I was famished. I savored every bite of dinner exactly as if I had been through exactly what I had been through. I carefully calculated what food in front of me would transport discreetly for morning. Before saying our farewells again, the Captain was interrupted with a subordinate's whispered message, and he then invited John to step out on deck with him.

There, in a ten-gallon hat, tall as anything you see in wild west posters, complete with waistband holsters and bullets and guns, stood the vigilante, holding up a small and very drunk and crumbled-like-a-puppet Colombian, wanting to find the sailor who could identify the wristwatch he found on him. John wanted to know about the notches on his guns—sure enough; one for every man he killed in the barrio he guarded when the sailors were in town.

Well, that calls for one more drink for the road, I insisted. I slept fitfully till the long, low horn of a ship broke the midnight silence. Could that be our ship leaving, I asked myself? I struggled off the lumps, looked out through the broken wooden blinds and saw our ship moving slowly and majestically out to sea. Words cannot express the total forsaken and abandoned emptiness I felt as the only link to civilization slid away. Tears fell fast, silently at first, then a controlled ache took over and I stoically got through till the morning train started us up the mountain.

One year later, I was delighted when John invited me to join him on a boat trip up the San Juan River into the Choco rain forest in the jungle of North Colombia. Splendid idea! Not knowing anything about boats, I thought nothing when John mentioned "harbor boat for 5 days." Well, sleeping might be cramped; it won't be the Grace Line, I thought, just some river cruise ship. And anyway, anything remotely resembling above standard was by now as instinctively alien to me as unbottled water.

We flew to the coast in a light plane and went directly to our boat. Well, yes, it was small. But what a marvelous opportunity to be part of a pioneer expedition, searching for new hardwoods to market. As I was introduced to the other members of our group, I noticed the huge books being carefully carried by the two botanists and two entomologists. It would later fascinate me to watch them every evening, meticulously photographing and logging the various rare plant and insect species they had discovered on land that day and spread out on the only table on deck. Everyone shared their excitement. The many jars of formaldehyde would finally be capped as we braced ourselves before going below to the stifling galley for dinner. And we were always hungry; the satisfying dinners—mostly fish we caught the last few nights—were unadorned as meant for the hungry.

The one covered room on deck provided adequate protection from storms. At one end was a sitting area with a large U-shaped wooden bench with a back. The ample deck had a single shaky rail with the bare necessities such as lifesaving equipment, conceding obvious defeat to the elements of nature on a tropical coast bordering a jungle. A lifetime of service preceding its Colombian ownership, it sat obediently, gray and faded-looking, on the murky water that never had a chance to clear between the dark downpours. Its shallow draft was clearly designed for the harbor duty of servicing navigation signals; it certainly had never needed sleeping quarters.

I was thinking as I looked around, eager to check out our cabin, that it was a good thing John insisted we travel light, as that narrow stairwell (actually a ladder!) would allow only a small suitcase. Wrong again—we then learned that below was nothing more than the galley with our dining table and the one toilet stall. Any bathing would be done with the hose on deck, in bathing suit, and with soap if you had any. Thus did we ten passengers, cook and crew live together for five unforgettable days, drifting on and off the shores of the rain forest.

Edith, the only other woman on board, John and I were the lucky ones who got to retire each night to the U-shaped bench; everyone else had his hammock or sleeping bag on deck. Each of the three sides was long enough to stretch out on. The bath towel I brought served as a pillow, but I had to forego using it to dry off after hosing and drip dry instead. The bench was paddable with our clothing, sometimes laundered on deck with soap and hose. Sleep mercifully won the comfort battle, almost always.

It was more depressing than the heavy air after the downpours to think about the living condition contrasts between the honeymoon cruise and this one. The heat, day and night, was sometimes so suffocating that my sweat felt like heavy metal. Liquid intake became just that; more a habit than refreshment. After my first shower on deck I discovered the hose water was just the river water pumped up—after that, to dirty my laundry with what I dirtied my body with was easy.

Every morning we would sail up the river some before dropping anchor to let the scientists go ashore, breaking through the thick jungle with machetes and wearing gathers on their ankles, which gave me the creeps if I thought about why. The air would become so still that even a dull knife could produce a clean slice. I knew the daily downpours between brilliant sunbursts would do nothing to cool us off, and thought moving up the river again would bring a breeze, which never happened, but which continually tricked me into thinking it might. I later thought the optimistic trickery was a survival instinct.

I don't think we could have endured the trip without the genuine camaraderie of all our boatmates. Nature has a winning way of stripping away all differences among humans willing to cooperate with each other through hardships. The last evening on board was a great example of our fun together when the cook announced we were down to only one egg. One of us instantly asked him to bring it out. We placed it in the center of the table, adorned with ruffles of paper napkins, after which we broke into song in Spanish, to the tune of "O solo mio": "*Un solo huevo!*"

The fascination of being so remote, the remarkable dampness and hidden noises of life, and the feeling of never having ever been anywhere else were suddenly interrupted when we saw canoes approaching with what seemed the strangest specimens yet—humans! In crudely made dugout canoes were multi-colored painted faces surrounded by massive heads of coarse, straight black hair and many necklaces of bright beads above loincloths. Except for obvious breasts, the women were indistinguishable from the men. Their smiling approach was a relief, as the jungle instinct of either hunting or hunted seemed already in our pores. Then we realized they were drunk, as they proceeded to act it, showmanlike, both in and out of water.

I was as eager to end this trip as a champion would his losing race. As we approached the last hours before arrival at dock back in Buenaventura, news reached us that the last plane of the day would take off early due to the pending storm, and we would have to overnight there. The news shocked me instantly.

"Oh my God! This can't be happening!" My horrible memories of the Hotel Estacion a year ago nearly knocked me over. A sudden ironical exclamation—"I know a great hotel; even has a star!"—somehow escaped my lips. Beyond that unexpected spark of life I was too tired to react beyond the disappointment of yet another day challenging my perishing civility, so eager to survive just days ago.

Entering the familiar hotel entrance, I only remember waiting in the background before a half turn found me following John upstairs, as the clerk's voice trailed behind: "Sorry we can't give you a better room, but we are always busy Easter weekend".

The first thing I saw as we entered our room was a fan. I didn't notice that it was noisy and rusty, as I had the one on the veranda a year ago. I was instantly drawn to it like a paper clip to a magnet. With strong arms outstretched beyond the walls, I looked around smiling. How happy I was to have a room to ourselves! And a real bed! This is great! As John explained that we had to share a bathroom down the hall, I instantly knew I would have the luxury of a real shower as I dashed to eagerly get what was left of my bar of soap.

What? An inside room? No need to even see the port then, much less hear a ship horn, I thought, as I ran down the hall to my heavenly shower. Being back in civilization felt good already.

PART IV
Family Life

Proactive Parents: Educating Children Abroad

by Pat Olsen

If you didn't expect to be a proactive parent, get ready to become one. Proactive—"acting in anticipation of future problems, needs or changes"(Merriam-Webster)—describes your role as a parent, one where you must fully engage in your children's education as your career leads you and your family to adventures in many countries and many schools.

You're all in this together

Education decisions are linked to the assignment process. No one in the State Department assignment system has the responsibility to tell you that a particular post might be a poor choice because of schooling. Education opportunities vary widely from post to post and parents need to research before bidding. The Department's Bidding Tool provides short descriptions of schools at each post. Check the Office of Overseas Schools website and contact their office with specific questions. Many overseas schools also have their own websites. Include your children in the decision-making process and keep your family goals and priorities foremost.

Elementary-school children overseas often develop acute skills of observation and analysis because they frequently have to adapt to new situations. One student commented, in reply to his father's apologies for again having to start at a new school, "Dad, starting a new school is no big deal. I'm a pro." While not all children will say this, many do feel that the effort required to transition to new schools in new cities is balanced by the opportunities and adventures that are the fun part of living overseas.

The issue of planning a move when your kids are in high school is a tougher but inevitable one, given the realities of the Foreign Service assignment system. You probably can't get each child through an unbroken four years in a single school. Many posts do not even have suitable high schools. Requiring your children to be part of the discussion and research, giving them input and some control in the assignment and school decision-making process will facilitate their adjustment to change. Many students find it easier to adjust when they move with siblings and so provide each other companionship during the no-new-friends-yet period. The last-child, senior-year move would seem to be the worst of all choices; but it too can be handled by most seasoned FS children.

Taking the road well-traveled

Foreign Service posts located in larger cities around the world typically have one or more English language K-12 school available. Posts in smaller cities have fewer, sometimes no options. Look at each school's accreditation, curriculum and philosophy carefully. English language schools may identify themselves as British, American, or international, which will be reflected in the program they offer. Ask your hometown principal for your school's grade-level curriculum to help you understand what your child would be learning at home, or refer to the Virginia Standards of Learning, available for K-12 on the Virginia Department of Education website.

Some international schools are adopting the new Primary Years Programme (PYP) for ages 3–11, and the Middle Years Programme (MYP) for ages 12–16, developed by the International Baccalaureate Organization. The goal is to provide a framework for an integrated curriculum, using units of study that include several disciplines rather than studying each subject separately. The framework incorporates global themes appropriate for classes comprised of diverse and internationally mobile students. Learning is based on the student inquiry model, where the learner takes an active role in building his or her own understanding. Each school develops its own curriculum around this framework. Although this teaching methodology differs from the standards-based model increasingly used and under debate in the United States, inquiry learning and an integrated curriculum are well-respected educational concepts and practiced in many U.S. schools.

High school programs usually include either the Advanced Placement Program (AP, a U.S. program of the Educational Testing Service), the International Baccalaureate program (IB, the Diploma Programme of the International Baccalaureate Organization) or both. Both the AP and the IB are rigorous examination-based university preparation programs for students in the final two years of high school. The AP program is a series of optional, advanced level courses offered within a general high school curriculum. The IB differs in that it is a comprehensive two-year curriculum, with a set sequence, offering some student choice of subjects within the curriculum. Some American high schools now offer the IB, so American universities are very familiar with it and readily accept high school credits earned by IB students.

Many international schools offer grade 13, corresponding to other national education systems that include an extra year of high school study. The two-year IB may therefore be offered in grades 11 and 12, or in grades 12 and 13. Keep in mind, though, that Foreign Service dependents are authorized education benefits only through the equivalent of twelfth grade. Students earn credit for IB courses actually taken even if the student completes only one year of the program.

If you are considering enrolling your children in a British school, note that students in British schools usually enter grade one a year earlier than students enter U.S. schools, so the grades may not correspond. Be sure your child is placed correctly by age and academics, not just by numerical grade level.

Overseas schools generally do not offer the same range and depth of resources beyond the classroom that are available in most suburban U.S. schools. If your child has severe learning problems, most overseas schools will not have the resources you need. Accordingly, if you have a child with any specific educational needs, be sure to contact each potential school by phone before putting the post on your bid list. Be honest and straightforward about your child's needs. Refer to records from your previous school. The administration will be able to tell you about the school resources available and whether your student's needs can be accommodated.

New kid in school

If there is a choice of schools at post and you can make a decision only upon your arrival, let each potential school know your plan. Schools will work with you more happily if you work with them. While many schools have arrangements where U.S. government dependents are accepted regardless of date of application or enrollment caps, it is not in the student's best interest to show up unexpectedly and be given a seat that the director has had to scramble to find. In addition, this agreement does not mean that the school is obligated to accept a child whose needs it determines it cannot meet. Unlike public schools in the United States, private overseas schools are not required to meet the educational needs of every child who wants to attend.

One benefit when attending an overseas school is that your child is not the only one who moves from school to school. Highschoolers, particularly those who have spent long periods overseas, note that it is often easier to transfer into an international school than an unfamiliar stateside high school. At the international school, everyone knows what it's like to be new, few students have gone to school together for more than a few years, and the school culture values and accommodates transient students.

Find out the starting date of school and, if you are going to the southern hemisphere, when the school year begins. Many schools have a special introductory day before the official start of school. Visit the school ahead of time, before it is crowded with kids on the first day of school, so your child becomes acquainted with the physical setting, and has an opportunity to meet some of the staff, without the pressure of opening day.

Some schools require placement testing, an interview, or both. Bring school records and share them with the administration and teachers; too often, records are carefully filed and the teacher—the person who needs to know your child's background—never sees them. Bring health and immunization papers. Find out what other documents the school may require and bring them with you—all in your hand-carry luggage.

Meet the teacher ahead of time if you can; at least plan to meet him or her in the first weeks of school. Discuss your child's background, strengths and weaknesses to help the teacher get to know your child. Raise topics of special concern right away. Ask about the teacher's style, classroom and school expectations, homework, lunch, and social events. Ask about the role parents can play at school and the systems for school-parent communication. Not every school has a parent-teacher organization or other mechanism for this important link.

Don't let needs identified or progress made in one school be lost as you transfer to another school. It will take the teacher time to get to know your child. Few of us have flawless kids who fit perfectly into every school, every classroom, even if we were to stay in the United States. Keep evaluating your kids over time, looking at the needs of each individual, to be sure they are thriving in the overseas lifestyle.

Be sure that your child has adequate and appropriate social opportunities. Many overseas schools pride themselves on being a close-knit international community of teachers, students and parents, welcoming and integrating families into the school milieu. The expatriate community or your local neighborhood may offer additional opportunities to participate in activities such as sports, scouts, and music programs.

Taking the road less traveled

What if you are interested in an overseas assignment where there is no appropriate school for your children? Should you consider unusual options? Possibilities including homeschooling, schooling in a language other than English, and boarding school, require personal, family decisions based on a family's priorities and goals. Don't forget that each year of childhood is a period of significant physical, mental, and emotional growth and development. Your child deserves that each year be as rich as possible.

Homeschooling is an option frequently considered since its recent rise in popularity in the U.S., but few families ultimately choose to homeschool overseas. All family members must be seriously committed to making homeschooling work. Many choices of homeschooling curricula are available, as well as online resources and support. Educators consider homeschooling an option generally most appropriate for elementary level students for a limited period of several years. It can be done; the author's family would have missed a unique Pacific atoll experience if they hadn't chosen to homeschool for two years.

Some parents give serious consideration to enrolling their young children in a school in the local language, whether or not a suitable English language school is available. Educational research shows that early language acquisition is key to command of a second language. Find out the experiences of other parents who have chosen a similar alternative. The family's future plans, the individual culture of a school, and the age and nature of the student are all important considerations in determining whether a student will benefit from the experience.

Lack of a high school at a potential post raises the option of boarding school, which in turn raises several factors a family needs to consider together. Is the student ready to be away from home for extended periods? Are parents willing to have their child living away from the family? What is the distance between post and school? Evaluate the location of a school in terms of emotional distance as well as travel distance. Boarding schools each have their own atmosphere; the family should visit a school before choosing to enroll their child. Although at authorized posts the government allowance covers basic schooling costs and transportation, the boarding school milieu, depending on the school, can impose additional costs for activities and general student lifestyle that may strain family financial resources. Ask families with boarding school experience to discuss it with you and your student.

Rough spots

The unexpected is part of the Foreign Service. We keep a packed suitcase under the bed, hoping we never have to grab it, but occasionally we do. Evacuation from post is always disruptive, but it becomes more difficult if you have school-age children. Depending on the situation at post and the length of time anticipated before return, the children may need to attend a U.S. school for an indeterminate, almost certainly disruptive period that fits no academic or personal schedule. If one parent remains at post, the family will have additional stress. Each family has to make individual plans according to their own resources and preferences, and based on a bewildering array of questions and U.S. government regulations. Mid-year transfers, planned or unplanned, are also disruptive. The children have to leave one classroom midstream and then jump into another that is already in progress with friendship bonds and academic routine already well-established. Sharing the first and last days of school are rituals that are important to kids, even if they may be too young—or too old—to tell you so.

We say goodbye to many friends in a career of moves. It can be especially hard for children to understand the constancy of friendship. Electronic communication has dramatically changed our ability—and our children's—to keep up with friends as they or we move around the world. Encourage your children to keep in touch with a few close friends. Correspond by e-mail, plan visits, send pictures. It is important for our children to know that friends we make on one tour are not gone forever. It does require effort, though, even for adults, and kids from grade school to high school need to be reminded and helped to make that effort to stay in touch. If you move from the country where your highschooler graduated or spent most of his or her high school years, plan, if possible, to send him or her back the following year to see friends and enjoy the return to a familiar environment. Knowing that they will go back for a visit helps ease the pain of transition and missing old friends.

One of the educational challenges for families overseas is making sure your children become proficient readers. Current research shows the importance of reading to your children from infancy. This means bringing with you and constantly ordering a wide variety of books in English to maintain and challenge your young readers' abilities and interests. Libraries even in large overseas schools can't compare with the resources available in the United States, and English-language resources are likely to be limited at post. Look for suggested age-level reading lists, available from home libraries or schools. Share hand-me-down books with other families. Encourage grandparents to send books. Spend time in bookstores when you visit back home. Coordinate with your child's teacher to support your child's reading program. Overseas families often have more time to spend together, with less intrusion from television, so there is ample time for both reading together aloud and independent reading. Be sure to give your young children lots of time with books and with you, especially if you have a non-English-speaking nanny.

Summers always bring choices to be made—to stay at post or return to the States to visit and stay with family for several months. Summer activities for kids can be hard to find overseas, especially if there isn't a parent free to stay at home. Older students want jobs, but may have few or no options. Parents and kids face a dilemma when college students, who may not even know anyone at post, need a home for the summer but also want to be employed and earn money.

End of the story?

A parent's greatest task—and greatest worry—is to ensure that our children, growing up in the Foreign Service lifestyle, develop into happy, knowledgeable, perceptive, and culturally adept children. All members of the family will be involved in the process—asking endless questions, experiencing adjustment and self-doubt, making difficult decisions, and juggling competing needs within the family. New Foreign Service parents can draw some comfort from learning about the strengths children can develop and carry over into their adult lives by reviewing the research on global nomads, children who spend at least part of their lives overseas because of a parent's career.

Most of us do manage to educate our children successfully with the normal amount of highs, lows, worries and proud moments along the way. Most of us raise our children in ways different than we were raised. We can't give them the life we had growing up. We can't give them the security of a hometown, the familiarity of one local culture, the context of neighbors they've known all their lives. We give them instead very different experiences, ones we hope they appreciate and that will prove to be a rich, wide-angle world experience with other cultures, peoples and languages—in short, a foundation for wherever they choose to go in their own lives.

Many of us come to understand what the life we lead has meant to our children when we read the inevitable college application essay "My Hometown," and see our young adults thoughtfully attempt to express who they are, how they got there, and what value they place on their unique childhood. After reading each of our three children's essays, we had tears in our eyes and knew that despite the moments of uncertainty and difficulty, each of us treasures our adventures as a Foreign Service family.

Educational Resources

Advanced Placement Program of the Educational Testing Service: **www.ets.org**
Global Nomads: **www.globalnomads.association.com**
The International Baccalaureate Organization: **www.ibo.org**
U.S. Dept. of State Family Liaison Office: **www.state.gov/m/dghr/flo**
U.S. Dept. of State Direct Communication Project papers:
      Resource #30 The Home Study Option
      Resource # 35 The Boarding School Option
      Resource # 36 Special Needs Resource Information
U.S. Dept. of State Office of Overseas Schools: **www.state.gov/m/a/os**
Virginia Department of Education: **www.pen.k12.va.us**

Tales & Travails of Teenaged Daughters in One Foreign Service Family

by Jan Zatzman Orlansky
and daughters Tamar Weisert and Robin Joy Orlansky

This essay is not a guide for parents of teens who are serving overseas; rather it is a series of "snapshots" of one family trying to navigate the labyrinth of choices available to teens and their parents and how our family addressed some of these choices. As the title suggests, there *are* travails along the way, which all families experience to some degree, whether overseas or at home. Our daughters are 21 and 26 years old now and have their own unique perspectives on their lives as teens living abroad. You will also hear their voices (in italics) in a kind of point-counterpoint discussion.

We entered Foreign Service life when our daughters were 9 and 14 years respectively, and the only other foreign travel, apart from visiting my family in Canada on vacations, was the half year we spent in Zagreb, Yugoslavia (Croatia), where my husband was a Fulbright scholar. The girls were 3 and 8 years old then. This experience proved to be a seminal one, because both daughters had positive memories of living in Zagreb and traveling around Europe. Six years later, when we discussed the possibilities of living overseas, they had only positive memories. We really didn't have to "sell" them the idea of leaving the security of their school, home and friends. They were ready, and in some ways they were more ready than their parents were!

One misconception we had about the Foreign Service was that our children would become worldly and possibly make friends with local children. How naïve we were, looking back on the past twelve years. First of all, our children as teenagers and their friends rarely, if ever, became close friends with children in the host country. Secondly, we have observed that teens tend to mix with those from similar backgrounds. So the Koreans stay with the Koreans, the Americans with other English-speaking teens, etc.

My observation is that the younger children mix more readily with a variety of children from other countries and as they mature, they mix more with those who share similar backgrounds. This is an unfortunate phenomenon, but being aware of it from the outset might help parents make choices that bring different groups of teens together. I have serious doubts, however, that much can be done to reverse this phenomenon, for one very fundamental reason. Teens are trying to figure out who they are during this emotionally and physically tumultuous time in their lives, and it takes a secure and well-grounded person to reach out and make an effort to get to know someone on a personal level, from another culture. As far as worldliness is concerned, our children do have a better understanding of different cultures than most of their American counterparts. However, because of the necessary restrictions placed on them as foreigners in countries that were not always safe, they were not able to take full advantage of learning from and interacting with the people and culture around them.

I had a wonderful experience at the Jakarta International School (JIS) ; I met my 3 best friends and my husband there. I think that the friendships you establish while at an international school are stronger than others are because you have shared such a unique experience. I am as close as I am to those friends not only because of the history we have together, but because we are able to relate to things that people who have not lived overseas would just not understand.

There are certain foods or smells that may seem very different to most people, but can take us back to a familiar time and place. We understand that as a foreigner in a third world country, it is not unusual to have maids or cooks. It was not strange to us to hop on a plane to visit our parents halfway across the world for Spring Break. We were Americans in a culture which was not our own, but one that on a certain level, we grew very comfortable in. I remember coming back to the States for the summer and feeling a type of culture shock at how bright and white and clean everything was. In a way I grew to prefer the atmosphere of the third world because I had grown used to it. There is definitely such a thing as "third-culture kids"; you can't claim to be a part of the culture of the host country you're living in, but you also don't quite fit into American culture. To some people this may be an unsettling way to grow up, but in my case, at least, it allowed me to form amazingly strong bonds with the friends who shared this lifestyle.

Jakarta, Indonesia was our first post, where the Jakarta International School helped nurture both girls with an excellent academic curriculum and a positive social outlet. They both thrived during our three-year tour there. Since our elder daughter graduated from JIS, the first big decision that we had to address was where she would attend college and this process began at the end of her sophomore year.

Before leaving on R&R during the summer break, we gathered information on a few small liberal arts colleges which we intended to visit. The main point of the visit was to give our daughter the opportunity to be interviewed and to tour a few campuses. We did the same thing at the end of her junior year with a closer eye toward colleges that were her top choices.

We did not fully realize how much our younger daughter would miss her older sister when she went off to college, but when we arrived in Ghana, West Africa for a two-year tour, it was on the eve of her thirteenth birthday. We wanted to have a birthday party for her, but she did not know anyone yet to invite, and it was not a happy time initially. She was teary-eyed and, when asked what she wanted for her birthday, she said, *my sister*…and so it was that we got our African bush dog "Dogma," not exactly a substitute, but a loyal companion, nonetheless, for the year our younger daughter was with us. This brings us to the second big decision that we had to make overseas.

Living in a "greater hardship" post can take on different meanings, from security risks to a lack of basic amenities, and in the case of Accra it was the latter, namely a lack of a good international school. As an eighth-grader, the quality of my education was not a particularly high priority, but my overall quality of life was of course essential to my happiness. Since the majority of my time was spent in school then, the lack of after-school activities and the general problems that come along with having a 15-person middle school (lack of resources, etc…) ended up being the impetus for me to move away from my family for my ninth grade year. This does not mean that I was miserable for the one year I spent in Accra. On the contrary, I was lucky enough to find a group of close friends from school that I would play with after school and on the weekends—usually swimming at the pool or beach, or jumping on a friend's trampoline—and I was overall carefree and happy.

When people ask me today "what was the best country (Indonesia, Ghana or Guatemala) *that you lived in when you were growing up?" I often reply with "I can't answer that, because I was at such different stages in my life at each of the three posts." I had a fun year as a 13-year old in Ghana, where the local people were friendly, the culture vibrant and exciting, and I had good friends to play with after school. I believe that if I had stayed there another year, however, or if I had moved there when I was older, I would have been very bored a lot of the time.*

At that time, the Lincoln School in Accra did not have enough students to have a curriculum with many options. Our younger daughter was in need of more stimulation, and we had to find a school that would challenge her academically. In Ghana we did not have Internet access to information in 1993 and had to send away for information, fill out applications and wait for their responses-a rather long and tedious process. She was applying for ninth grade. Since we were so far away, the schools she selected interviewed her over the phone. The Putney School in Vermont was her final choice, in part because they took the time to call her and ask her about her life and what she enjoyed doing. In addition, a Putney student called and introduced herself saying that she was looking forward to meeting our daughter. It was a warm and welcoming beginning and when we took her, along with her older sister, to Putney, it was clear that she would be embraced by the faculty, staff and students, and be well taken care of. That did not take away the enormous hole in our hearts as we said goodbye to our almost-fourteen-year-old daughter and drove our nine-teen-year-old daughter to the airport to catch her plane to Colorado College.

It was a dark moment for us, as parents, when we then headed back to Ghana to complete our second year of the two-year tour. Putney proved to be a wonderful choice for our daughter. It is a farm school with high academic standards that prepares its students well. The students grow, harvest and can their own vegetables as well as rotate farm duties for each student. In addition to a strong academic curriculum, they also have a strong extra-curricular program, in which our daughter fully participated. The following year we moved to Guatemala and our younger daughter accompanied us to that post, where she completed grades ten, eleven and twelve at Colegio Maya, the International School in Guatemala City.

I was offered the position of College Counselor at Colegio Maya. Knowing how sensitive teenagers are about having their parents within earshot of their activities, I thought it prudent to discuss this job offer with our daughter first, who would be seeing me every day in her small school. She was not thrilled with the idea! No tantrums, no sulking, just a look…**the** look that speaks volumes. I suggested that there be a trial period during which time she would let me know if my presence at the school was impeding her social life. The short story is that she and her friends would come to my office frequently during those first few weeks of "the trial period" and for the three years that followed, not only for college guidance but also as a stopoff point between their classes, just to chat.

Our next post will be without our daughters, but an interesting twist to this story is that our son-in-law, along with our elder daughter and their baby daughter, is considering a career in the Foreign Service after passing both the written and oral FS exam. Our younger daughter is working in Japan. Does FS life replicate itself within Foreign Service families? That would be too simplistic to contemplate, but what it does do is open up the world to children and teens to choices that they might not otherwise have considered, had they stayed in Anytown, USA.

Shallow Roots: A First-Hand Perspective on Not Staying Put (our younger daughter)

While I know that spending my formative years (ages 10–18) abroad has been a trade-off for not having close childhood friends, and for getting tongue-tied at the question "where are you from?" I believe that the benefits far outweigh the costs of my upbringing. The impact that growing up overseas has had on my life is ever-present in my life as an adult. Having spent so many years living in exotic third-world countries is not simply an experience that I can look back on as a phase in my childhood, but rather an upbringing, which has effects that have permeated into all the veins of my life.

When I was actually living abroad with my family, I didn't often think about the exceptional circumstances under which I was living. I went to school every day, participated in after-school activities, and hung out with my friends like teenagers in most countries of the world do. When people today ask me, "wasn't it hard for you to move around so much?" I explain that it was never particularly taxing on me, because I just accepted my life as it was, without questioning the transcontinental leaps I was making every few years. Of course I was aware that my counterparts in the United States were staying in the same place, with the same friends that they'd had since nursery school, but the fact was that overseas I was attending schools with people in similar situations as myself. This is not to say that moving away ever became easy. By the third move I realized that the students and teachers in international schools were generally very accommodating to transferring students, and that I would always make at least a few close friends very shortly after arriving in my new home.

The impact that moving around so much has had on me shows itself now in my apparent inability to stay in one place for more than a few years. As is the case with a lot of Foreign Service kids, I'm considering a career in the Foreign Service or some other internationally-minded organization for myself. In fact, I write this composition from my current home in Japan, where I came to teach English directly out of college. Growing up overseas and moving around so often was clearly not traumatic enough to prevent me from pursuing a similar lifestyle of my own volition!

The Plight of the Pantoflarz: Trailing Husbands in the Foreign Service

by Douglas Kerr
Warsaw, Poland

Pantofel is the Polish word for a woman's high-heeled shoe, and a man living under a woman's heel" is called a *pantoflarz*. The mildly saucy imagery of the hen-pecked husband as "gigolo" or "boy-toy" is fully intentional. So is the sarcastic humor, and in this way Poles have successfully devised a term for "trailing" or "dependent" husbands. Poland is a traditional, Catholic country with conventional social stereotypes. In the U.S., too, the traditional "Ozzie and Harriet" stereotypes survive. Father still knows best, and when he walks in the front door and calls "Honey, I'm home!" he expects to see his apron-clad Donna Reed-like wife sweeping towards him, martini in hand, for a peck on the cheek.

But the times they are a-changin', and in the Foreign Service, just as in the rest of American life, there is an increasingly large number of trailing husbands. The AAFSW even changed its name to recognize us. Embassy Warsaw in Spring 2002 has seven trailing husbands. Statistically, given the size of this post, that's not far off the census average.

How are we *Pantoflarzy* doing? In preparation for this essay, I interviewed the other six trailing husbands here. We comprise a varied group. Of the seven of us, three are employed, even lucratively, outside the Embassy, one is self-employed, one is applying for a range of

Embassy jobs and will most likely be employed before you read this, and two have decided to be stay-home dads with their preschool-aged children. Our ages range from mid-20s to late 40s.

Yearn though we may to live in a gender-neutral world, unfortunately we don't. And we are all conditioned by societal gender-role stereotyping. Generally, these men face the same issues as accompanying wives, and many of their comments will resonate with FS wives. Their attitudes towards the lifestyle hurdles are perhaps slightly different because of societal conditioning. Consequently, so are their approaches to tackling these issues. I'll come back to this point in my conclusion.

The questions I asked these men fell into three general areas: 1) Biographical information. I was curious to know how long these couples had been together, and, especially, how long they had been in the FS. 2) Employment issues. I asked about previous jobs and careers and what these men have been doing with their time overseas. 3) I asked general questions about how they are treated by Embassy personnel here and at other posts, and by federal government personnel with whom they've had contact. I concluded each interview by asking for general recommendations, and advice for any male partners considering joining this lifestyle. Here are our stories:

"Derek" was successfully employed in a high-tech field when he met his FSO wife. He was 39 and had been working for an agency that placed him with companies needing his skills. After ten years in his profession, he had come to be quite well-paid but was "ready for a sabbatical." Derek's wife, a tenured mid-level officer, is on her fifth assignment and her third overseas tour. They are now the happy parents of a vivacious one-year-old, and in the next few years there may be more children. Derek, now 42, made some big decisions: he gave up a career to accompany his wife overseas, fully in the knowledge that he would be "Mr. Mom" for a few years. He is seeking to maintain his skills, but with only some success. Unfortunately, the fast-paced nature of technological change means that his skills are slowly atrophying. He knows that were he now to seek work in his area, as he says, "it would be really easy for me to find a job, but for less money," since he would most likely be hired as an employee, not as a contractor again. But his old career, he says, was "high-paid blue collar work" and lacked the full range of rich experiences available in the Foreign Service, which he has come to relish.

Derek has participated in baby groups organized by the international (women's) groups here. He first went with a "trailing wife"—someone he'd met in language training at the Foreign Service Institute. Her friendship made it a little easier for him to be the only man present. But he says he didn't feel particularly awkward or uncomfortable. That is a tribute both to his strength of character and to the receptivity of the women in the group. He says he enjoyed meeting women from several other European countries; he found them interesting and benefited from the social contact. Since he has recently taken a part-time job at the Embassy, he no longer attends, but he feels comfortable with his social life, and knows that if at any time he felt a great urge to meet new people and make more friends he could do so. He's aware that the social organizations overseas are generally oriented toward women, but acknowledges that "I don't mind having it harder for us."

Though he is a quiet soft-spoken man who might appear shy to some, Derek doesn't lack self-confidence. He's clear about the choices he's made to put his career on hold and become a Mr. Mom, and is happy with both his decisions and the reasons behind them. He, like many associated with the FS lifestyle, recognizes that money is far from the only goal in life. He's content not only with the personal, familial happiness he's found, but also in the wide range of opportunities and experiences available living overseas. He's optimistic about his future and ready to welcome whatever the future brings. He has a range of ideas he might seek to pursue in the future, some but not all of them involving work. He has an easygoing attitude to FS life, and warns others "not to fight the system." For those husbands and couples considering entering the FS, he cautions that if continuing a "location-dependent" career is a high priority for the trailing spouse, then "a tough decision must be made." Although he thinks the 1950s social stereotypes are fading fast, he recognizes that the FS life is one where it is extremely difficult for both partners to pursue careers, and says (ominously) of the lifestyle: "don't [try to] make something work that wasn't designed to work."

"Vincent" and his wife have been doing just that, and with some remarkable success. But their streak may be coming to an end. He is a 34-year-old international lawyer who has been able to continue to work in his field overseas. His wife is a 35-year-old tenured mid-level officer. They have been together for five years but have known each other for eleven. For the first part of their five years together, Vincent and his wife lived in the U.S., both working in Washington D.C. and New York. Before moving overseas, Vincent had already become well established with his law firm, and they were happy to have him continue working on international issues while being posted in Europe. Now he's nearing a point in his career where he can expect to become a full partner in his firm.

He is about to take on a large responsibility elsewhere in Europe, and his wife will take leave without pay to accompany him as he does so. Vincent is very well paid. It's unclear what Vincent's wife will do in the future, but it is certainly a possibility that if his career continues to blossom, the federal government may lose her. This would be a tragic loss. She is a fully-trained, highly competent, experienced mid-level officer, in whom the government has much invested. She speaks several languages and works in an understaffed cone. Were she to resign, it would be a regressive step for gender equity in federal service.

When asked about the way he has been treated by the Embassy, Vincent notes "They assume the spouse is there as a dependent spouse" and that they "express initial surprise" when they find out he's not. That strikes Vincent as oddly anachronistic. Nonetheless he has enjoyed the FS personnel he's met, noting that they are great people, fun and intelligent. However, in his experience, they "expect that one spouse is going to give up everything for the other" and that has inevitably caused problems. He remarks that the government has not shown as much flexibility in accommodating their dual careers as he had hoped it might. The private sector, he feels, does a much better job at finding compromise solutions to difficult issues such as this. Consequently, it is able to avoid the worst-case scenario of losing a well-trained, experienced professional like Vincent's wife. This may be a case where the private sector, with its eyes on the bottom line, a board of directors and a group of shareholders, is motivated to act with more accountability, and thus perhaps more rationally, than government.

"Ray" and his wife are overseas for her only FS assignment. They both have had full careers in the military. Ray, 47, retired from the Army ten years ago, but he has been anything but a rocking chair jockey since then, staying active in his professional field. He has been stationed overseas in Asia and Europe, and says that after twenty years' traveling he just feels tired. Ray and his wife were on the brink of packout when I interviewed him, and they are looking forward to returning to the U.S. Before arriving at post, Ray was able to get hold of a listing of American Chamber of Commerce CEOs here, and he mailed his resumé to all those he thought might be interested in his talents. Then, happily, "the calls just started coming in" and he had secured a very lucrative job in his area before arriving in the country. Not only has he reaped substantial financial rewards—"I get paid really well," he says—but Ray has also been able to watch the transition of a post-Communist economy from the inside. He has enjoyed the feeling of "building something new."

Ray talks of the parallel career paths he and his wife have pursued as though they each take turns. He says of the past three years "this is her time, this is not my time." This seems slightly self-deprecating, since Ray has been highly successful here. Indeed, he notes, "I could stay here and be an expat, and she could turn around and be the spouse for a while." In social settings, Ray, like most of the other men in this group, feels quite comfortable, "because I hold my own," but this implies he'd feel less comfortable if not employed, or as well paid. Perhaps he feels men who are not making money are less likely to "hold their own" socially.

Ray has enjoyed this overseas posting, saying "this is living large; we don't pay anything but the food and the phone." Yet, when asked what advice he might give to a hypothetical young dual-income couple considering following in his footsteps, he confesses he would have to discourage them. Ray and his wife have been exceptionally successful in making the dual career path function overseas, if only for one tour. But for most couples, Ray says, one partner must usually agree: "OK, you build your [career] and mine will suffer" for a while. Ray would agree with Derek's caution not to try to make the system do something it wasn't designed to do (the larger question, one for a different essay, is: Can the system design be improved?). But Ray and his wife are an example of one of the best possible outcomes of trying to make the system do something it wasn't built to do.

"Malcolm" exemplifies another possible outcome. His situation has much in common with Vincent's and Ray's. He was a journalist in the U.S. and was able to make the international transition and keep working successfully in his field. But he has some reservations and regrets. Malcolm is 31. He and his wife have been married for three years, together for nine. His wife is a first tour junior officer (JO) at a Consulate. He resigned from a D.C.-based NGO to accompany his wife overseas. Before leaving the U.S., he, like Ray, tried hard to secure a job. Unfortunately he was unable to find one in the same city as his wife, but was successful in finding employment elsewhere in the same country. Consequently Malcolm and his wife have lived apart for two years. He was dissatisfied with the job search information and help he received from the diplomatic community, which he found "limited" and in some respects "patently untrue."

Partly because of Malcolm's employment and career goals, his wife's next post will be in D.C. And in the future, if his wife stays in the FS, his employment needs will be a "huge factor" in their bidding. He speaks of their continuing in the Foreign Service as no more than a possibility, and not a probability. If he is successful in finding a good job in the U.S., his wife will quit the FS and re-enter the private sector. Malcolm remarks, "While I don't expect the Foreign Service to act as a placement center, I think it should consider that dual-career couples are quite common in modern-day American life and work to send those couples to appropriate posts." When asked about PIT and PSC Embassy jobs, Malcolm replies, "I have no desire to work in a secretarial position at an Embassy or Consulate, and my wife doesn't expect me to." Like all the other husbands, Malcolm has found Embassy personnel to be thoughtful, accommodating, and helpful. Institutionally, though, he says "it seems the Foreign Service thinks all families are like the Cleavers, from *Leave it to Beaver*." When asked to give advice to a hypothetical couple considering joining the FS, Malcolm's advice to the trailing spouse is to "check your aspirations." He thinks it is extremely difficult for both partners to pursue full, rewarding careers overseas.

"Barney" and his wife are on their second overseas tour. Both now in their mid-twenties, they were originally high school sweethearts. After losing touch with each other for a while, they reconnected in an Internet chat room. Romance blossomed, and they married. Alas, Barney's experience on their first overseas tour could hardly have been much worse. He had been well-employed in the U.S., saying "I was very well paid." He had been unable to take language training before leaving for post. That was only one reason (but a major one) for his unhappiness there. He says he never left the house in two years, and felt depressed: "I didn't know my place." He feels he received the cold shoulder from the trailing wives at post: "I never heard from one single spouse."

Now at their second post, Barney is trying hard to avoid a repeat performance. He has benefited from the language training he was able to take at FSI and feels confident in attempting to speak the language in everyday situations. Barney and his wife live in a downtown apartment and he enjoys getting out, walking around the city center and getting acquainted. As well, he is enrolled in a university course and is able to study online, which is keeping him occupied. He is applying for various Embassy jobs, and is determined to find at least part-time work. The chances that this tour will be a happier and more successful one for Barney are fairly good, though much will depend on his ability to find work. He is prepared to accept even relatively menial secretarial positions as a stop-gap.

For the longer term, Barney has ambitions to join the FS himself, most likely as a specialist where he might be able to use his area of expertise. Barney says "We've kind of set ourselves an ultimatum: if I'm not in the FS at the end of this tour, [my wife] will leave." The overall trailing husband experience for this couple, them, has been mixed at best. When asked if he would do it all again if he had the chance, Barney says flatly "No." His advice to newcomers to the FS in his situation would be to try as hard as possible to learn the language, and to apply everywhere for every job going, to build up your collections of movies and books, and to be prepared not to hear from Embassy wives.

Lastly, I'll come full circle to the second Mr. Mom I interviewed. Drew is 33 and his wife is a 32 year old first tour JO. They've been together since 1998, while Drew's wife was a stay-home Mom to their two preschool-age kids. She had always toyed with the idea of taking the FS exam, and after she did, and passed, they slowly came around to the idea of playing the role reversal game. In the U.S., Drew had been a very well paid software developer with an Internet start-up company. He and his colleagues, some of them 'Net millionaires, rode the stock option bubble all the way up, and all the way back down again. Nonetheless, when his wife joined the FS and he quit his job, the family took a substantial cut in income. But Drew describes their initial time at FSI as "great." He enjoyed being the stay-home Dad while his wife was in language training, and he enjoyed having her home early each day. In the D.C. area he would take his kids to play groups, and says he "didn't feel uncomfortable being the only man in the room." He says there was no gender-based tension. In fact, he says, he thought the groups found it "more interesting because I was a man, like it was cute."

Like Derek, Drew seems comfortable with his decision, and is enjoying spending time with his kids. And again, just like Derek, Drew is a man who has enough self-confidence to play Mr. Mom for a while. After two more years, when both kids are in school, he may look for work again. While working at his old Internet company, he felt uncomfortable bearing the responsibility of supporting a family of four: "I had trouble being the main breadwinner; I was nervous about losing my job." For Drew and his wife, these are early days in the FS, but at the moment everything looks rosy. He's delighted with the housing, the neighbors, and the FS so far: "There's no hidden secret. Everything I was told before is even better than I thought it would be."

I can't postpone my turn any longer. I'm 39, and married to a 41-year-old first tour JO. We've known each other for twenty years and been married for 18. We spent many years together in graduate school. When my wife accepted a job as an English Literature professor, we bought a huge old Victorian house that had seen much better days and I worked full-time to restore it. We had two kids, who grew up watching Daddy change diapers in a tool belt (on more than one occasion those diapers were held together with duct tape). Along the way, a woodworking hobby blossomed into a small business. When our youngest child turned two, I took out my first business license and became sole proprietor of a part-time custom cabinetry shop. My first commissions were architectural millwork jobs for friends who'd witnessed my work on our own house. My wife's teaching schedule allowed her to be home in the afternoons, and I found time to work then, on weekends, during naptimes, and during the half days our youngest was at school. We sold the Victorian painted lady when I finished it, and sank the proceeds into a house in the country with a huge garage/workshop for me. Then my wife joined the FS.

I was originally more strongly predisposed to the FS than she was. We had lived in the same small town for ten years and were ready for a change (she had taught *Macbeth* twenty times, for example), but for her it wasn't easy to resign her tenured faculty position and give up stability and the only home town our kids had ever known. I knew that my occupation might not be easy to take up overseas, but I was willing to try. I had a prescient hunch that expats might be a better market for me than the Ohio community where we lived, nestled in one of the holes of America's Swiss cheese economy. After arriving at post and receiving our HHE, including most of my power tools, I set up shop. Soon I found clients, and so far things have gone about as well as could be expected. A key goal in trying to run a woodworking business overseas was to avoid boredom. If anything, the opposite has been true, and I feel constantly short of time. I've also been able to undertake some freelance writing and editing for the Warsaw Stock Exchange.

I have more experience at the role-reversal, Mr. Mom game than any of the other men discussed above. For ten years I have been the "primary caregiver." I did attend playgroups in the U.S. and overseas. I'll confess to feeling the tiniest bit of unease in "rooms full of women," but in the U.S. the source of that unease was at least as much because of my British accent as it was because of my gender. Overseas, I attended an International Women's Group playgroup with a former Marine Security Guard turned Mr. Mom, and we lent each other moral support. On one occasion, that support was a little more than moral. My MSG pal was physically assaulted by a mad Russian angry at where he had parked his minivan. We hustled five kids under five into their car seats and hastily retreated from the scene, my friend reminiscing about the three-second barehand kill he still remembered, and how tempted he had been to use it. Perhaps it's worth noting, in a chapter on role reversal, that in some ways it makes sense for a wife to work in the safety and security of the Embassy, and hubby to be out facing the physical perils we sometimes do overseas. When, a few months ago, I stumbled upon a gang of car thieves in the act of stealing our car and was Maced, one of my first reactions was relief it hadn't been my wife doing the grocery shopping that day.

Like the other men interviewed, I've not noticed any "strange" reactions from Embassy or other government personnel. Both the Embassy and the State Department do attempt to assist accompanying spouses. I have received the Ambassador's permission to run a home-based business. The Embassy has hired me as a contractor on a few woodworking jobs, and that has certainly been appreciated. I was also offered an Embassy PIT job, but during the five months I waited for DS to process my security clearance, my custom cabinetry business took off. I have since declined the Embassy job, which would have paid me only about $350 per pay period. I can top that. And, at least as importantly for me, I'm able to set my own timetable, and I do something I love. I'm still the family's backstop in case one of the kids is sick or needs a ride, and I enjoy the fact that working for myself allows me to do these things, or, for example, to accompany the third grade field trip to the zoo. I'm the one that sees the kids off to school in the morning and welcomes them home in the afternoon. I believe strongly that in expat communities where the gender roles tend to be the more traditional ones, it's important for other young children to witness a father being a "room Mom" or "field trip chaperone."

For the future, I'm cautiously optimistic that I'll be able to keep woodworking overseas. Much depends on the housing, the electrical system, and the local market. But trees grow almost everywhere, and wooden furniture is always in demand. I take great pleasure in confronting and surmounting the challenges of trying to run a small business here. Recently I was delighted when a local tool sharpening service allowed me to start running a tab. I feel thrilled when I'm able to overcome linguistic and other hurdles. Some months ago, before setting out to buy some cherry lumber, I looked up a few words and phrases in my dictionary and had noticed that one of the two words for cherry was denoted "vulgar" but had neglected to mark which one on the notepad where I'd scribbled them both down. So, with fingers crossed, and figuring I had a 50–50 chance at getting it right, I sauntered into the lumberyard practicing the Polish phrases for "Please, Sir, show me your cherry"; "Please, Sir, how much is your cherry" and "Please, Sir, I want to buy your cherry," all the while prepared to duck a possible right hook to my jaw from the burly foreman. When instead he burst out laughing, I knew I'd picked the wrong word, but that all would be well. Since then, Pan Bogdan, assured of his day's entertainment, is always happy to greet me.

I agree with many of the comments of the other husbands above. It's vital, I think, to remain flexible, and open to whatever opportunities may present themselves. It's essential to have a range of fallback plans too. My freelance writing and editing fits into that category. There will usually be opportunities to teach English overseas. Taking as much language training as possible is very important. Certainly a "location-dependent" job presents the trickiest issue. All of these comments could apply equally to accompanying wives. Like the other men, I feel fairly comfortable in social settings here, but in part I know that this is because I too "hold my own."

I can't help wondering how male FSOs who feel condescension toward Mr. Moms might treat their own wives and the wives of their colleagues who are at-home Moms. Condescension towards primary caregivers who don't work outside the home does not contribute to healthy relationships, no matter what the gender roles are. Life overseas tends to exaggerate these types of strains, because of the absence of familial and other support, and because of the language barrier.

Conclusions: "Hire the Soldier, Retain the Family"?

It bears repeating that employees' husbands face many of the same issues and difficulties as employees' wives. The employment, language barrier, and domestic isolation issues are similar for both husbands and wives. But wives often have a social support network available at post that is not always as readily accessible to husbands. Life may be slightly harder in that respect for men. On the other hand, there is no evidence in my admittedly small sample anecdotal empirical evidence to support the contention that men find it easier than women to secure Embassy jobs, an opinion expressed in the trailing husbands chapter of Katherine Hughes' excellent book "The Accidental Diplomat."

The husbands I surveyed have each approached the trailing spouse issues in subtle but importantly different ways. Those husbands who've had the most success to date are the ones who initially recognized the full scale of the difficulties they would face and that they alone would have to surmount those obstacles. Derek, Ray, and myself, although each of us with remarkably different goals, have so far been successfully living the trailing husband lifestyle. But Vincent, Malcolm and Barney, who each in their own ways expected more help, flexibility or support, are the ones who are less than fully satisfied, and who are finding less than full success as trailing husbands. Drew's experience is too short to form a valid basis for conjecture.

Perhaps it's one of those sad but true observations that, like a child on Christmas Eve who doesn't really expect Santa to bring that huge, expensive new toy, those of us with more realistic expectations are less often disappointed. But the most important caveat here is that the husbands who expected little or no help from the Embassy or the federal government at large took it upon themselves to be independent and autonomous self-starters. Ray is the best example of this. Initially recognizing the scale of the hurdles results in greater success overcoming them. It's a more easygoing approach to assume that "this is her time" and "I'll pick up whatever work I feel I can" overseas. This attitude has conditioned the job search and career goals of these men. And that conditioning has paid off, in some cases handsomely. Knowing that they would have to beat the bushes for any and every opening, they have arrived at post predisposed to do so. They hit the ground running, with a fully formed assessment of the difficulties they would face.

All of this can be said of trailing wives too. There are both women who have met with success as "trailers" and others who have been less happy. The more successful and happy wives tend to be the ones who have found their own way. Those who've hoped for more institutional support or help have sometimes been disappointed. But there may also be a genuine gender-based difference in the dynamic being played out. Trailing husbands overseas experience a greater degree of separation from traditional gender norms than do trailing wives. They are able to leverage that freedom and independence into developing successful paths for themselves, whatever those paths may be. The men I interviewed each spoke of experiencing this feeling to varying degrees. They all mentioned a sense of freedom and opportunity, and a lack of constraint. Trailing wives are not as far removed, overseas, from traditional gender-role stereotyping, and perhaps it tends not to be as easy for trailing wives to recognize the range of choices and opportunities. Perhaps trailing wives are less reluctant to ask for help and support from the Embassy community than trailing husbands, and therefore wives are more vulnerable to disappointment if it doesn't materialize.

The above comments suggest that female FSOs whose husbands have well-adjusted expectations might even as a group be able to make a more successful transition from life in the U.S. to life overseas than male FSOs. But it must be emphasized that of the seven couples discussed in this article, three will probably not stay in the Foreign Service, and a fourth couple, Ray and his wife, had only ever planned a single tour. Of the remaining three couples, Drew and his wife are so new to the FS that it's hard to speculate about what their future holds. Perhaps only two of the seven couples can be said to have a fairly strong commitment to life in the FS. Again, of course, seven couples comprise too small a sample from which to extrapolate. But it would be shocking if that ratio, or anything close to it, exists across the ranks of the FS. The State Department should investigate that question. The Department's Diplomatic Readiness Initiative attempts to address the problem of attrition by massively increasing the number of new hires. Attrition should also be addressed by shoring up retention of those already in the FS. Increased retention could be achieved with only a little more institutional flexibility and a little less inertia. The loss of female FSOs like Vincent's wife is an enormous tragedy.

Malcolm commented that he didn't expect the Embassy to act as a placement service. But the State Department has tried to address the spousal employment issue before, and is doing so again. Embassy Warsaw is one of a handful of posts selected to pilot SNAP (Spouses' Network Assistance Program) whose goals are not so far removed from those of a placement service. One other point: when an Embassy is considering contracting out work in an area where a freelancing spouse already operates, every effort should be made to give the freelancer preferential treatment. There are, unfortunately, anecdotes of Embassies preferring to give contract work to individuals on the local economy, because locals usually cost less (but not if the cost shows up in the FS attrition rate). *Fly America* requires the government to use U.S. airlines. EFMs receive preferential hiring for Embassy jobs. The international schools hire Embassy spouses. So contract work should, where possible, go to freelancing members of the Embassy community. Every post should maintain an up-to-date skills bank of its community, and, wherever possible, try to place contracts within the Embassy community. EFMs hired for Embassy jobs should receive a level of pay commensurate with what those jobs would pay in the U.S. One senior Embassy wife commented that the Embassy's HR department knows it can pay us poorly "…because they have us over a barrel." We get nowhere by abusing our own.

Should the State Department consider the career needs of the spouse on at least an equal footing with, for example, medical clearance, language needs, and children's issues when making assignments? Is there not a position somewhere for Vincent's wife in a city where an international law firm could be found to make use of his talents? Is there not a post for Malcolm's wife where an experienced professional journalist and editor could find a position on the local economy? Of course there is. And the Department could find those posts for those couples. The Department's standard reply to these questions is that every additional criterion factored into the assignments process inevitably makes the process a little more unfair for other officers who might be denied plum appointments as a result. This is true, but it is also a prevarication. When it suits the Department's own goals, it is happy to introduce such additional criteria, and prepared to live with a skewed process. Take, for example, the case of tandem couples, or the case of officers with special needs children.

All that remains, then, is to convince the Department that it is indeed in its own best interests to account for spousal career needs in making appointments. In doing so it would tackle what may very well be a large rate of attrition among female officers, and a large, hidden, gap between the level of commitment felt toward the FS by female and male officers. There is a need for a Department-wide study of these questions too.

I'll end with one last point. There are in the U.S. today millions of talented, capable, married women working outside the home. This is a huge pool of talent which the FS too often leaves untapped. Married men in dual-income couples are more likely to apply to the FS than are married women. The "mommy-track"—a function of our biology—means it's easier for couples to see themselves in the FS for at least a few, child-bearing and child-raising years, with women in the role of primary caregiver. Social stereotypes also mitigate against married women in dual income couples joining the FS. These professional, competent married women tend to gravitate away from the FS because of their husbands' careers. Were they instead to sign on with Uncle Sam, they would contribute to the Diplomatic Readiness Initiative's success. Addressing their concerns with their husbands' careers need not be an enormously difficult or expensive process. Secretary Powell has on many occasions repeated an Army mantra: "hire the soldier, retain the family." All it will take is a little careful thinking outside the box.

If the U.S. government wants to present a true picture of America to the world, it must encourage these women, and these couples, to more seriously consider joining the FS. On this topic, as in so many others, the government seems a little tardy in catching up with broader society, and with the private sector. The 1950s have long since receded from view in the rear mirror. The Cleavers have been put out to pasture.

Letter to a Foreign-Born Spouse

by Margaret Bender

Although there are no statistics, it is estimated that between one-third and one-half of the spouses of employees of the foreign affairs agencies of the United States are foreign-born. This letter contains advice gathered during interviews with over 40 foreign-born foreign service wives and from my own 25 years' experience. Many of the concerns of the foreign-born mirror those of the American-born: frequent moves, lack of employment, less-than-desirable recognition and support. But other issues are of particular importance to women who have left their native countries, and therefore their support networks, and followed their American spouses to the United States and beyond.

While most of my conversations have been with women, I know that there are many male foreign-born spouses. To avoid the "him/her, his/hers" problem in writing, I refer here to the employee as male, and the spouse as female. However, much of the information applies to male as well as female spouses.

◆   ◆   ◆

Dear Foreign-born Spouse-to-be:

Congratulations on your engagement! You are about to embark on a way of life that is interesting and often exciting but one that requires patience, perseverance, and a sense of humor.

Before your fiancé can be given permission to marry you (and still keep his job), your background will be investigated thoroughly. You will be interviewed, as will members of your family and other people who know you.

This is the time you should do some investigating of your own. If at all possible, travel to the United States to meet your fiancé's family and friends. See him in his own environment. Also visit the Washington, D.C. area because this is where you will live while your husband is on a home assignment.

Be aware that the housing your fiancé enjoys overseas is sometimes larger and better-furnished than his salary will afford in the United States. His position and representational duties abroad are taken into account when this housing is assigned to him. In Washington, he is responsible for finding and paying for his own housing and furniture.

Before leaving your country, collect all your official documents: your birth certificate, baptism certificate, academic diplomas and transcripts, employment records and references, and anything else of an official nature that you may need to produce at some later date and which would be difficult to obtain from abroad.

Have frank discussions about money. Although financial matters may not be discussed openly in your culture, in the United States it is more common that couples manage their finances together. As many marriage counselors in the United States agree, money management is a topic that should be clearly understood and agreed upon by couples planning to marry.

Keep records of how much money you bring to the marriage. You should know how much your husband earns and what his debts are. Your own debts should also be discussed. You should have direct access to the family finances even if you do not hold a paying job. Try to establish credit in your own name through a credit card or department store account in the United States. Be careful with your credit. A poor credit rating can mean refusal of mortgage and other loans.

It is also a good idea to have an emergency fund set up in your own name. In the event of marital problems or divorce, you don't want to be stranded without money. Before you have a green card or a social security number, you can open an account in your own name with the branch of the bank in the State Department, provided you and your husband maintain a joint account there.

It is no longer required that you become an American citizen (unless your spouse works for one of the intelligence agencies). If you do not, you will not be issued a diplomatic passport and will travel on the passport of your home country. You will not be eligible for certain jobs in the American Embassy. At the time of writing, the security clearances of dual-nationals are being reviewed with the possibility of the same restrictions being applied to them as to foreign nationals.

If your husband is employed by the State Department and you do decide to become a naturalized American citizen, you and your spouse should contact the Family Liaison Office (FLO) for assistance with expeditious naturalization. In spite of its name, this process can take months. Employees of other foreign affairs agencies should contact their own offices for guidance.

If you are not already fluent in English, written and spoken, make that your first priority. In order to function independently, and especially if you want to work in Washington or in an Embassy, you need to be able to communicate well. Some foreign-born spouses have a good command of spoken English but cannot write well enough for employment. There are many low-cost options for language instruction in the Washington area. Your spouse's professional proficiency in your mother tongue should not take precedence over your learning English. Insist on speaking as much English as possible at home. (If, on the other hand, he does not speak your mother tongue, encourage him to learn it. He can't understand you properly unless he understands your language and your culture.)

Learn to drive. For Americans over the age of 16, this is almost as common as walking. You may come from a large city where public transportation is commonly used, or from a country where hired family drivers are the norm. There are many suburbs in the Washington, D.C. area where public transportation is inefficient and in order to move about independently, you will need to drive. Most newcomers to Washington find the traffic daunting, especially on the Beltway, but you will adjust with practice. The ability to find your way around by car is especially important during times of evacuation. Women who have usually relied on their spouses to drive them everywhere find themselves stranded when evacuated to the Washington area on their own.

Don't depend on your spouse for all your information. Take as many classes as you can at the Transition Center at the National Foreign Affairs Training Center (NFATC) (formerly called the Overseas Briefing Center at the Foreign Service Institute) in Arlington, Virginia. Each fall, two courses are offered there that are of specific interest to foreign-born spouses. One is on cross-cultural marriage and the other on transition to Washington. Sign up and take your husband along with you. He will benefit from the discussions as well.

Learn for yourself the rules and regulations of the Foreign Service that affect your life. For example: household goods stored in the United States at government expense will have the employee's name on them. For you to access your personal belongings, you will need a Joint Property Statement, signed by you and your spouse and notarized. Before leaving on an overseas assignment, make sure that you have a copy of this form and that one is on file in the Transportation Department. Always remember that the State Department's first loyalty is to the employee.

While no one expects you to turn into an American overnight, learn as much as you can about the history and current events of the United States. Not only will this help you to understand your new community, you will feel better prepared to participate in discussions, especially overseas.

The first time you come to Washington on assignment, think carefully about where you want to live. Many women said they felt stranded in outer suburbs that emptied every morning as their neighbors went to work. Living near a metro station allowed them to move about more independently if the couple had only one car, which the husband needed to get to work.

A Washington assignment is very different from one at an Embassy. There is no self-contained foreign service community to welcome and support you. You will be expected to function much more independently. While your spouse is on a Washington assignment, make friends with people where you live who are not in the foreign service. Having a network of contacts (through a church, a club, or neighborhood association) that is more stable than the mobile foreign service community will be of great help while you are living in the Washington area or should you return in the future in an emergency.

As you learn more about the United States and become more comfortable in Washington and in an Embassy community abroad, don't neglect your own culture. Seek out people who speak your language and maintain those cultural ties that are emotionally important to you.

Contact the Foreign-born Spouse Group through the AAFSW. This is a friendly, informal group of foreign-born foreign service wives who meet monthly in members' homes. It is an excellent source of information and support, especially in the beginning when you will have many questions. Reach out and ask, don't sit at home, lonely and isolated.

Welcome, and good luck! You have lots of company.

Foreign Service, Commuter-Style: Maintaining Long-Distance Relationships

by Sheri Mestan Bochantin

One of the lifestyle options available to many Foreign Service couples and families is that of the separated relationship. Whether by choice or because of a lack of options, many employees, especially couriers, Diplomatic Security special agents, rovers, technicians, and others might find themselves doing an overseas assignment without their loved ones, or maybe they just travel away from home base a great deal. Whatever the reason, there are things that can be done to set realistic expectations and ease the pain of the separation...*and* the reunion!

To start off on the right foot, whenever possible, the decision to take a posting that will separate the family should be a joint decision. The reasons for choosing to live separately cover the board, from financial gain (an unaccompanied tour to a danger post pays well), the spouse's employment situation at home, medical concerns, or maybe family issues, such as elderly parent or special educational needs for a child. When all parties are involved in the process and buy into one of these reasons, there will be less opportunity for blaming and misunderstanding when the going gets tough.

Partners should evaluate the strength of the relationship before deciding to make the separation. Those who are most successful in this situation have respect for each other, a good level of trust, and a strong commitment to the relationship. It's also useful to have been in the relationship a year or more, though many new romances have begun as the employee was shipped off, and have survived a few months of long-distance romance before getting back together.

An assessment of the involved personalities is also in order before making such a decision. Are you able to live alone and be independent? Do you have a sense of adventure and a willingness to do something unconventional? You must be confident that you can make the relationship work, and have a capacity to make the commitment. Certain abilities are required: to be a planner, organizer, to be creative and flexible, and have the memory to remember what is really important to you. You must have a good sense of humor—even a sense of the absurd! These traits will make the rough spots a little smoother for you.

Once you are in the separated relationship, there are certain red flags that you must avoid. Don't leave any unfinished business between yourselves just to avoid unpleasantness. Make sure you have uninterrupted quiet time alone to discuss everything.

The relationship will require constant vigilance; don't become complacent. Watch out for love saboteurs—family members or friends who may unconsciously or consciously try to break up your relationship, maybe because of envy, loneliness, or a sense of being threatened. Be aware of outside distractions to the relationship. If your mate mentions feeling threatened, pay attention. Don't minimize that concern; just because you don't think there is a threat doesn't mean that it's not real to your partner.

Decide how much time apart your relationship can bear, then try to see each other as often as needed for both parties. The same goes for communication, however that may take place. This aspect can be eased somewhat by your willingness to put money into the situation—paying for airline tickets, getaway weekends at a midpoint, and ridiculous telephone bills have saved many a Foreign Service relationship.

Be aware of the stranger factor: going through the motions of a relationship but not really connecting. Speak up if you feel alienated. Figure out what's dividing you and work to reestablish intimacy.

When the children grow up and leave home, it can hit a couple particularly hard if they are also apart. The spouse no longer has caregiving responsibilities at home and the traveling employee may feel guilty for not spending more time with the kids. It is also intimidating to have to start treating each other as a couple again instead of parents.

Be careful that one party does not become overburdened with the sole responsibility of childcare, household duties, or financial matters.

When one party or both become tired of the travel, problems arise at work or at home, or there are issues with the children, it's time to reassess the situation and decide if the relationship can still withstand the pressures of a separation.

Just as in regular cyclical moves in the Foreign Service, long-distance relationships have phases: leave-taking, being apart and re-entry. How can the pressures of leaving show up in our relationships? Petty bickering, crying easily, and looking forward to departure—all of these incidents are symptoms of separation anxiety. Understand why you are picking on each other and you will be less likely to let the little fights get to you after you separate. To cope with departure, it's useful to set up rituals that work and go through them each time. However, be prepared for the fact that you might not have time for any romantic little rituals—the fancy candlelight dinner you lovingly prepare the night before the big split may be ruined by a late night in the office closing out files and packing boxes.

In short, acknowledge that the separation does hurt, don't leave unfinished business, cry together if needed, and don't make light of your partner's needs.

You have to shift gears when you are apart, to become single again. This is also a point where many get scared when they realize that the other party has also just become single again! The imagination can start running away with you when your partner is not home for that weekly phone call you had planned. There are positive coping methods you can use at this point. Anticipate that you will feel lonely, but realize that we are often alone throughout our lives, not just this moment. If the loneliness does become overwhelming, get out and help someone who is truly lonely.

Focus your energy on maintaining the relationship across the miles, which is where that creativity comes in handy. Find interesting ways to stay in touch with each other, and remember that frequent letters, packages, and flowers in the office will point out that there is someone somewhere in that person's life—make them know you care, and let everyone else know it too!

The biggest fear we have about a commuter relationship is that old "absence makes the heart wander" adage, but research says otherwise. A study done at the University of Maryland in the mid-80's showed that only eight percent started an affair after separating for work-related reasons, but 11% of those who had been having an extramarital relationship stopped it when the commuter situation began. Why? We don't tend to get bored with each other or take each other for granted. We may be doing this for career enhancement and that absorbs all of the energy. Traveling can mean hectic schedules and jetlag—not conducive to "shopping" for someone else.

As for reconnecting, it takes time and patience to adjust to being together again. We expect to feel sad, lonely, or uncomfortable in the leave-taking phase but not when you get back together. It is a jolt to the system when those emotions hit. In fact, it is quite similar to the culture shock we feel when we move back home.

The traveling party must reestablish his/her territory upon return, getting familiar with the surroundings again, and possibly questioning why things have changed in his/her absence.

The couple will have to shift gears and change social patterns again; getting used to doing things with someone else requires a change in mindset. We also must change roles—you will become a spouse and parent again, not just the employee. The single parent will be able to share the responsibility again, a prospect that can be disconcerting for children and parents alike! Your lifestyle may also change—it may be more laid back or faster-paced than the previous separate routines.

You must be realistic in the romance department when you get together. While it may be like a honeymoon every time, it may also be a letdown—jetlag, work pressures, and domestic duties are not the greatest mood-setters!

These strategies work for Foreign Service families in various scenarios, whether you choose to take the unaccompanied assignment for a year in a danger post, you have to be on the road two hundred days of the year, or you are involuntarily separated by an evacuation. The same tools that are essential throughout your Foreign Service life—good communication skills, flexibility, and a sense of humor—will come in handy in the long-distance relationship as well.

Just a Gay Spouse (JAGS)!

by Nam Nguyen

To call myself a gay "spouse" of a Foreign Service Officer (FSO) would be a misnomer—the word *spouse* implies a married man (in my case) with legal recognition and protection under law. Gay and lesbian couples cannot get married in the traditional sense in the United States.[1] Not that I feel a particular need to be a "spouse," but I do feel strange being introduced at Embassy functions as my FSO's "partner," for lack of a better word. After being in a committed relationship for over ten years, and with four major moves among posts under our belts, being called a "partner" sounds a bit (dys)functional.[2] Foreign guests at receptions often miss the nuance of our familial relationship, and politely smile and shake my hand while wondering why my FSO has a *business* partner. Without an appropriate label to construct a group identity, much less a positive one, my fellow gay/lesbian "spouses" or "partners" are reduced to being an invisible minority within the social structure of the State Department. In an organizational culture that values title and status, where you stand is where you sit. Gay/lesbian "spouses" don't even have a chair to sit on.

Without legitimate status at State, gay/lesbian "spouses" have been ignored or deprived of the benefits normally bestowed upon their heterosexual counterparts. How often have Community Liaison Office

---

1. Vermont's civil union is in a class by itself.
2. I realize that the lack of an appropriate word to identify someone we love, who is a family member of our gay/lesbian household, is a larger phenomenon that extends outside the confines of Foggy Bottom.

(CLO) coordinators omitted gay/lesbian "spouses" from functions hosted by an Ambassador's spouse? Can the gay/lesbian "spouse" be considered for a job opening at post? Will the Ambassador or Deputy Chief of Mission (DCM) invite the gay/lesbian "spouse" to functions that include the spouses of heterosexual officers? For emergency evacuation purposes, are we always listed on the roster of family members as stipulated in the Member of Household (MOH)[3] guidance? I haven't mentioned the bigger items that a heterosexual spouse need not worry about, like diplomatic passports and immunity, health insurance, medical evacuations, home leave, travel and relocation costs, or education of adopted or natural children of gay/lesbian "spouses." But however small the questions above are, the toll of being treated as second class will eventually grate on the identity of the gay/lesbian "spouses," to the degree that, not being masochists, most choose not to participate in the communal life at post.

I have to fret over the smallest details when moving to a new post: will my possessions be shipped with my partner's? The most stressful issue in a new posting is to find a job abroad for the gay/lesbian "spouse," presuming you're not independently wealthy. Luckily, I found a job with an investment bank at our last post. My company solved the visa and work permit issue. Others are not so blessed. I have heard countless horror stories of how gay/lesbian "spouses" have had to resort to makeshift student visa arrangements or to accompany the FSO as a "butler" or "nanny," swallowing pride all in the name of love in order to be together as a family unit abroad. Gay/lesbian partners get no "black passports" since they lack diplomatic immunity. Foreign citizen "spouses" don't even qualify to naturalize and carry "blue passports" as U.S. citizens and so face still greater difficulties in terms of

---

3.   The Member of Household guidance, issued in December 2000, provides certain limited accommodations and assistance for members of FSOs' households, including unmarried partners, beyond "Eligible Family Members" (spouses, children and other direct dependents).

legal status abroad, depending on the host country's relations with the home country of the foreign "spouse."

Bidding and assignments give rise to much anxiety for gay/lesbian couples. With each move, each posting, the identity of a gay or lesbian "spouse" is tested or questioned. As my partner and I contemplate our[4] next posting abroad (after a wonderful and worry-free posting in New York), I have set only one criterion: I will not accompany him to post as his servant. Being Asian American, it just looks wrong!

I know of many gay/lesbian couples—and wonder how many more there are—who have been separated, or, worse, dissolved, because the "spouse" did not want his/her professional career to play second fiddle to that of the FSOs as they moved, on average, every three years. We can learn from our heterosexual counterparts, who have dealt with these issues for years—making hard choices between a career stateside and being a fabulous diplomat's wife/husband abroad. Gay/lesbian "spouses" can't even get that far along, without the visa to remain in our FSOs' countries of assignment. There's an unusually harsh, but truthful, saying among the gay/lesbian "spouses" that FSOs' pets enjoy better benefits, and thus respect, under Department rules than we do.

At the recent 10-year anniversary celebration of Gays and Lesbians in Foreign Affairs Agencies (GLIFAA), "the officially-recognized employee organization representing the concerns of gays and lesbians in the foreign affairs agencies,"[5] I met several new recruits, freshly minted from A-100 and openly gay and lesbian, who had previously resigned themselves to the single life when they decided to join the Foreign Service, given the difficulties for an accompanying partner under current conditions. What resolve to serve their country! To their amazement and mine, I will admit, there were lots of accompanying gay/lesbian "spouses" in attendance, not to mention those that were abroad at the time. GLIFAA estimates that there are dozens of gay/les-

---

4.   Of course, I have a say in the choices my partner includes in his bid list, a fact that narrows his options and could be detrimental for his career in the long run.
5.   The direct quote is from GLIFAA's website at **www.glifaa.org**.

bian couples serving abroad. For me, the amazement is not in that number today compared to, let's say, when GLIFAA started in 1992 or during the McCarthy years in the 1950's, but how the existence of these gay/lesbian couples in the Foreign Service proves that the strength of love and commitment can overcome harsh and unjust bureaucratic obstacles. It was a beautiful moment for me, seeing the new recruits realize that they can hope for a satisfying career and personal life.

But the Department's culture is slow to change. At a Foreign Service Institute Protocol Training course I once attended, I noticed that heterosexual spouses are also the target of bad manners; hence the dismissive and shameful phrase that they are "just a spouse." In the course, our first exercise was to simulate a cocktail party where you learn to hone your social skills by finding out facts about three guests and the name of the hostess. I had more interesting conversations with the spouses than with the FSOs. However, when an FSO found out that I was a "spouse", s/he would quickly back out of our conversation in search of someone more "important." Eventually, it dawned on me that I wasn't being ignored by the FSOs because I was gay; it was because I am "just a spouse"! Ironically, in a protocol training class, the FSOs failed the first rule of protocol: to avoid ruffling feathers. But then, who am I anyway? I am "just a gay spouse" (JAGS)!

JAGS of the World, Unite!

The Eighteen Cups: A Tale from the Medical Clearance Process

by Francesca Kelly

"I want a divorce," she said quietly. "I can't take this any more."

"You can't leave," he said imploringly. "What would I do without you? You're my soul-mate, the love of my life, the mother of my children, not to mention my..." and he began to sing, "Sex Bomb, Sex Bomb! You're my Sex Bomb! Baby, baby—"

"Stop!" she screamed. "Please, please don't do your Tom Jones impression! That just makes this even harder."

"OK," he said, holding out his hands in defeat. "OK, I know how hard it's been. All the moving, the new countries, the culture shock, the jet lag. But, listen, honey, I'll do more this time, I promise. I'll do all the paperwork. I'll arrange the packout. Hell, I'll even BE there for the packout! I'll do everything."

"Everything?" she asked sadly, pointing to the cups.

He looked at them—eighteen clean white paper cups, stacked up on the bathroom counter. "Oh, God, the cups. The cups." He sank into a chair and began to sob. "It's over. It's really over!"

Oh, hell, I'm not really going to divorce the guy; I love him too much. But right around moving time, which seems to happen every two or three years, I start with the heavy-duty fantasizing: about never packing out again; about going home to live in small-town, Norman

Rockwell America where Mom & Pop run the grocery store and every-one waves to everyone else, and there's a parade on July 4th with fire engines and town marshals.

And no one has to poop in a cup.

Somehow I always forget about this particularly unglamorous part of diplomatic life until once again, it's thrust right under my nose, so to speak. Just recently I came home with eighteen cups—three for each of us—and placed them prominently in the bathroom with a heavy sigh. The cups looked exactly like disposable coffee cups, complete with plastic lid, except that they had a 1950s illustration of a smiling, white-capped female nurse holding a clipboard in her left arm and some sort of vial in the other. Her expression was either warmly encouraging or annoyingly perky, depending on your attitude about medical tests, or, more apt in our case, on how long it took every fam-ily member to comply with her implied wishes.

We also each had three little vials to mix the, uh, cup's contents into. And a cute little card that tested for "fecal occult blood," too. And test tubes for blood lead poisoning and HIV, and slips listing all the additional things we'd be tested for at the lab.

Now, listen, I was grateful that the State Department was paying for all this; really, I was. But the fact remained that trying to get four kids to poop in a cup on three separate occasions was a bit daunting. If we had any diplomatic training at all, it got put to good use in this situa-tion.

"What? I'm not doing that!" was the shocked reaction of our teen-aged daughter.

"Yuck, that's gross," said our 12-year-old son. This from a boy who wouldn't bathe for a month if he had his choice.

And the twins, boys aged 7, simply thought I had to be joking. Oh, I wish.

I tried reasoning in a pleasant tone, and everyone nodded and seemed to understand. The cups were still there, unused, two days later. Next I delivered a demarche.

"If you want to go back to America this summer, you have to do this!"

"Why?" challenged one of the older kids.

"Because we can't leave Turkey unless we have our travel orders, and we can't get our travel orders until we get a medical clearance, and we can't get a medical clearance unless we poop in a cup three times!"

I don't even know if this is strictly true, but it sounds as if it is, and that's the main thing. It's a little like answering the three riddles of the Sphinx, or bringing in the broomstick of the Wicked Witch of the West, except harder.

In the first few days after the cups came home, my husband and I each dutifully performed our three small patriotic services for the government and took the vials to the lab, explaining that future deliveries—i.e., samples from our children—might be sporadic.

We turned our attention back to threatening the children. Threats turned out to be highly effective, although not in the way we expected. All four kids immediately became constipated.

Several more days went by, and one child even stayed home from school, he felt so ill. I thought these tests were supposed to help keep us healthy, not make everyone sick.

Meanwhile a dozen cups still sat on the counter, their pristine whiteness mocking us. Desperate, I brought out the last parental resort: bribery. A dollar a dump, to put it crassly. Do you know anyone else in the entire world—besides a farmer—who's willing to pay for crap?

My kids are stubborn, but they're not stupid. Let's face it, this was the deal of a lifetime. All four kids went for the money, and Round One of the Cup Saga was over. Only eight more samples to go. Whoopee. Preparing the four samples for the lab—which is ordinarily an odious task—I practically danced around the bathroom. That fact alone should probably alarm the State Department's psychiatric division, but I'm beyond caring.

Round Two: three out of four kids had to be reminded that there was easy money to be made, but after the reminder, no problem.

Fourth child—one of the twins—started digging in his heels as only a child can. I guess he somehow got the insane idea that his bowels and what they produce are his business and no one else's.

A day went by, and of course, the more we pleaded with our son to come through with the goods, the more he resisted. We could have conducted a graduate seminar in Child Psychology that week. He used the toilet at school, or at home when we weren't looking. He insisted it "wasn't the right time." He asked over and over again why he had to do such a ridiculous thing, when he'd already humiliated himself once. He tried all the arguments his seven-year-old mind could come up with, while we kept nagging, begging, scolding, yelling. These were not our finest hours as parents, believe me.

In the meantime, the other kids completed Round Three and upped their cash holdings at the same time. Naturally not everyone accomplished their assigned task at the same hour or even the same day. I made quite a few deliveries to the Turkish lab, where, every single time, we went through an Abbott-and-Costello-meet-Kafka routine of "Is this John's first?" "No, this is Will's third." "So this is also Annie's third?" "No, this is Joseph's second. Annie's done her three."

Finally it came down to our medical clearance hanging on the fourth recalcitrant child, who still refused to budge. The threats escalated. Now he couldn't play Nintendo, or have all of his birthday money. I'm sure his grandparents would not like to know that we held back their check to him for as long as he held back something else. They probably had this nice idea that he was feeling all warm and fuzzy about Grammy and Gramps as he counted his money and saved for a pony or something, instead of now permanently associating their gift with the production of feces.

Finally, on the eve of a special playdate with a friend that we said we might have to cancel (yes, I know, we are truly evil people), he came to our bedroom at 11:00 at night, clearly in psychological torment. With tears running down his cheeks, he said, "Mom, I did it, but I missed the cup. Can you fish it out of the toilet?"

I may be wrong, but I don't think this is covered in Dr. Spock.

I was able to make both my son and myself happy that night, although for once in my life I cheated on something: I used the results of my fun fishing expedition to fill two vials, and marked them with two different dates. I'd had enough of torturing my kid, frankly. And this was my decision to make, as my beloved husband never did prepare any of the kids' samples, if you must know. Kind of makes you think about adding a few lines to that pamphlet called The Role of the Foreign Service Spouse.

Now if you're another of the lucky Foreign Service parents wrestling with The Cups right now, and dreaming about living in Little House on the Prairie where they never even heard of stool samples or jetlag or travel orders, take it from me: This too shall pass. Everything will come out in the end. "It" happens.

*This essay first appeared on the AAFSW website, **www.aafsw.org**.*

PART V
Work and Technology

Surviving the Bureaucracy

by Mette Beecroft

Many who are considering joining the Foreign Service rightly try to prepare for this highly specialized existence by finding out as much as possible both prior to making a decision and also once they have committed themselves. Even if they have been thorough in their research, one reality of Foreign Service life for which people are often unprepared is the bureaucratic one. This is not to say that the Department of State bureaucracy is worse than the bureaucracy found in other U. S. Government agencies. However, especially for people whose only experience is with the private sector, the bureaucracy may seem unwieldy, irrational, inconsistent and impenetrable—all of which is to say extremely frustrating.

Expectations and timing are often part of the problem. The Foreign Service is very selective and expects people to adhere to the highest standards. Many who join have already had successful first careers. It comes as a bitter disappointment when the bureaucracy does not seem to be held to the same high standards as the Foreign Service employees whom it serves. Timing is also a complicating factor. Certainly when people first enter the Foreign Service, and later on at times of assignment to a new post, the stress level is high and time is always in short supply. Bureaucracies by their very nature move slowly and often only serve to increase the frustration and stress.

In spite of these unpleasant realities, especially once the employee has joined the Foreign Service, s/he can take steps to work within the bureaucracy.

Do not assume that the Department of State will take care of you. **The State Department cares well for people who first take care of themselves.** How does one do this? The answer: Assume that you have to be actively involved in all facets of your life—whether planning travel, managing a move, assembling information for claims or submitting a travel voucher. Keep complete records of expenditures. Make sure that you retain inventories from packing companies and storage companies. Inventory all of your possessions and videotape the more valuable ones so that you have valid proof of possession if you ever need to file a claim for loss or damage. If you are working with an individual to complete arrangements for something like a move, take the initiative yourself to stay in touch. You are always the best advocate of your own interests.

Take time to become somewhat familiar with the regulations—especially some specific portions of the Foreign Affairs Manual (FAM) and of the Standardized Regulations (SR). 6 FAM 100 contains all the regulations on Travel and Transportation and 6 FAM 300 regulates the functioning of claims. The SR codifies all the allowances. Some knowledge of these regulations will enable you to know what it is reasonable (or unreasonable) to ask for.

Bear in mind that regulations are not cast in stone. Just recently, Business Class has been made available to people traveling more than 14 hours on their way to a new posting. And frequent flyer miles earned through U.S. Government travel can now be used by individuals for private travel. The employee can now also be reimbursed for costs relating to shipping an animal. Become familiar with the independent groups at State which often advocate for change—the Family Liaison Office, the Associates of the American Foreign Service Worldwide (AAFSW) and the American Foreign Service Association (AFSA). Join them, support them, let them know what you think.

Develop a good network of people to whom you can address questions, whether about travel and transportation, personnel issues or allowances. What used to be very difficult to do has become much easier since we have e-mail, fax and usually very good telephone connections—even if there is a 12-hour difference. The reality is that some people know a lot more than others and some people care a great deal more than others. You can expect to get different answers from different people to the same question. Sometimes, people's answers to bureaucratic questions seem to be a function of their own personality. A generous and understanding person will use regulations to make things happen. A negative, uninterested person will use regulations to block action.

Especially at post, treat the Administrative Officer and General Service Officers (GSOs) as first-class citizens. I have encountered Foreign Service Officers who look down on Administrative Officers and GSOs because their work is not "substantive." Apart from the fact that condescension is not a likable trait, it is also an operational mistake to make people feel that you look down on them. A good Admin Officer or GSO uses regulations legally but creatively to get things done for you and for your post. A positive relationship with the Admin Officer and with the GSO will usually work to your advantage.

It is important to remember that bureaucracies usually function slowly. Though it is not always possible, allow enough time for the bureaucracy to function. Some parts of the Department of State move more slowly than others. At post, you can simply ask people how much time they think they will need, for example, to change your contributions to the Thrift Savings Plan or to get some information for you.

You also must recognize that at times, the bureaucracy will function poorly and it will inconvenience you. As I write, two examples come to mind. The Department recently announced that hard copies of Earnings and Leave Statements would no longer be issued since they were now available online. Unfortunately, they received at least 1,000 complaints in response, because the system was not working for employees overseas. In another example, the Department of State managed to acquire a private zip code for both individuals and companies who might send things overseas by pouch. Items bearing this zip code would not be irradiated against anthrax. Unfortunately, even if the United States Postal Service informed companies about the new zip code, it did not make its way into most business databases. Hence our private zip code was rejected as invalid.

Sometimes, these "mechanics" function very well. Other times, the employee and his/her family have to be prepared that they will not. Everyone has a horror story. The listener has to be prepared to evaluate the source and to keep things in perspective. The basic question is whether or not the many good things about the Foreign Service outweigh these sometimes unpleasant realities. We have been in the Foreign Service for some 32 years, so it should not be surprising that for my family and me, the advantages far outweigh the negatives. People who are flexible, who are determined to make things work and who are not especially self-centered seem to fare best. In spite of some unpleasant experiences along the way, I would not trade our Foreign Service existence for anything.

Foreign Service Spouse Employment Today

by Shawn Dorman

A June 1957 State Department publication, "Suggestions for Wives from Other Foreign Service Wives," offered the following advice:

"Being married to a man in Foreign Service gives you the satisfaction of using your mind and developing your capabilities in working more closely with your husband than would be true in some other occupations. There is a real job for you to do in supporting your husband's effort, and satisfaction in doing so. You can be a great help to your husband in his career, and can live a rich and rewarding life by helping him in serving our country."

The Foreign Service has come pretty far in 45 years for the Foreign Service spouse who wants his or her own career. But has it come far enough?

Back in 1957, the vast majority of Foreign Service Officers were men. Until 1972, spouses were considered government employees and their representational contributions were included in the FS employee's evaluations. A 1972 State Department directive ended that practice, leaving spouses posted abroad more freedom to host or not host representational events, but not, in many countries, free to find employment.

Until 1972, female FS employees had to resign if they married. Today, while the Foreign Service still has a male majority, the ratio is changing, and entering FS classes are more evenly split between men and women. September 2001 data from the department show that today's Foreign Service is made up of about 66 percent men and 34 percent women, out of a total of 9,333 employees. There are about 450 tandem couples in the State Department, and an additional 81 "interagency tandems," in which one spouse works for another foreign affairs agency.

Data from about 150 posts surveyed for the Family Liaison Office (FLO) Family Member Employment Report in 1999 showed that 55 percent of eligible family members were not working, 33 percent were working inside the mission, five percent held jobs in education, one percent worked for an American company, three percent were doing freelance work, and three percent were in other kinds of jobs.

Most FS spouses today are well-educated and, in many cases, just as professionally qualified in their own fields as their FS employee husband or wife. A survey from a few years ago found that 83 percent of FS family members had college degrees and 29 percent had advanced degrees.

Foreign Service spouses may be willing partners in the representation role and may spend some years not working outside the home in order to care for children, but they are less likely to sign on for a lifetime of non-employment than were the spouses of generations past.

Can A Foreign Service Spouse Have a "Career"?

As with so many questions about the Foreign Service, the answer is "it depends." An informal survey of FS spouses and discussions with Foreign Service officials concerned with spousal employment lead to the following conclusion: most FS spouses not part of a tandem couple will not have "normal" careers, but can, with a combination of the right skills and the right postings, have a series of rewarding jobs in their chosen fields, *if* those fields are ones that lend themselves to Foreign Service life. Almost all spouses will have inevitable gaps in employment as the Foreign Service lifestyle dictates frequent moves, as well as transition periods for training and home leave.

FS spouse and co-editor of this volume Melissa Hess suggests that a non-tandem spouse cannot have a career in the traditional sense, "but spouses can build a 'career path' by taking jobs in their chosen areas of interest, whenever possible." Hess has held many jobs teaching and training adult learners, and is currently the director of education and staff development at an Arlington hospital. Her overseas experience played a key role in landing her this job. She is also co-author of a book, *The Expert Expatriate*, along with fellow FS spouse and editor Patricia Linderman.

While some FS spouses find a peripatetic lifestyle either ends or puts a significant damper on a career, others, like Francesca Kelly, find it works well for those seeking less traditional careers. Kelly told us, "In many ways, I've actually found being an FS spouse an opportunity, career-wise, rather than a hindrance, but that's because I've never felt like a true 9-to-5-er and come from a long line of independent contractors, freelancers, entrepreneurs and starving artists. I also did not want to have to work when I started producing offspring, so being an FS spouse allowed us to live on one income and I have been able to be home for the kids."

Many FS spouses choose to stay home with children for some years. As FS spouse Jan Fischer Bachman notes, "If you want to stay at home with kids, the FS makes it possible because of perks like free housing. The stay-at-homers by choice are probably among the happiest group of FS family members."

Former Associates of the American Foreign Service Worldwide (AAFSW) President Mette Beecroft, who notes that she has "made a career of not having a career," explains that most FS spouses cannot have a regular career path in any occupation in which the work is anchored in a company or a place and in which there is a prescribed progression of positions. "If people are coming in with expectations of being able to have a regular career, they will be bitterly disappointed." Beecroft said that back in 1978, when she was part of the efforts that opened the FLO and established it in the department, she suggested to the board of examiners that recruits be told more about the reality of spousal employment. She remembers a negative response: they might lose people that way.

Today's recruiters, while anxious not to paint too negative a picture, are trying to provide more useful information so people can make the right choice about whether to join. Special Coordinator for Diplomatic Readiness Niels Marquardt says, "through pre-employment communications, we strive to portray to prospective employees the reality of spousal employment in the FS. We recognize this to be the leading issue for some potential recruits and have no interest in misleading anyone. We say quite honestly that 'the FS is not for everyone—but it may be for you.'"

Ray Leki, of the Foreign Service Institute's Transition Center, said spouses can definitely have careers, but those careers are "probably not going to be the ones they envisioned." He said that on the second day of JO training, representatives from the Transition Center and related organizations spend several hours with spouses. "We all want our new-hires and families to start out with realistic expectations, but this is an area of communication that is inherently problematic. It deals with aspirations and expectations that are formed without context. Most people will not have a good idea of what they are getting themselves into until after their first assignments."

Even though the State Department recruiting site has links to the FLO, and the FLO site does provide spousal employment information, many incoming FS employees still complain that they were not informed about the spousal employment situation. FLO's Employment Program Specialist Debra Thompson acknowledged this is still a problem and says FLO is currently putting together a special guide for the recruiting office to use in helping better inform recruits about employment options for FS spouses. It should be ready soon.

In early 2001, the FLO published the second edition of a useful book called *Employment Options for Foreign Service Family Members*, which provides information on job search techniques, portable careers and skills, federal government employment and other employment options for the FS family member. It is available in the FLO office and on the FLO website (**www.state.gov/m/dghr/flo**). The introduction is perhaps a little too rosy: "Before 1972, being a Foreign Service spouse was a career. Today, the question is not whether a Foreign Service spouse should have a separate career, but how the spouse manages a career along with the other requirements of the mobile Foreign Service lifestyle." But in the middle of the book, the section on portable careers gives a more realistic picture: "Since the definition of a 'career' means successive jobs with higher levels of responsibility and increased pay, few careers lend themselves to FS life. The best definition of a 'portable career' might be finding employment in one's area of training on a regular basis."

The Canadian Foreign Ministry is up-front about letting people know what the reality is for its Foreign Service. Displayed prominently on their website is this note about spousal employment, which seems just as relevant for its American counterparts: "Continuous professional employment overseas is usually not possible for spouses. In many countries, despite the lifting of formal barriers, it is difficult for spouses to find work due to linguistic and economic restrictions on the employment of foreigners. Some spouses find salaried work with an international agency, an Embassy or an international school; others do volunteer work or studies related to their careers or personal interests. Self-employment has been the approach taken by those with an entrepreneurial bent and portable skills."

The Bilaterals

In order for an FS family member to work legally outside the U.S. mission while posted overseas, a "Bilateral Work Agreement" or a "De Facto Reciprocal Work Arrangement" must be in place for that country. A bilateral is an official agreement between the U.S. government and the host country enabling family members to seek employment on the local economy. It is established through a formal exchange of diplomatic notes. At present, 84 countries have signed bilaterals with the U.S.

The de facto reciprocal work arrangement also allows family members to legally work on the local economy, but the permission is not based on any official signed agreement, but established by precedent. In these countries, there is established practice for family members to apply for and receive work permits. There are 53 countries with de facto arrangements in place. This leaves about 30 countries, in which we have a mission, lacking a work agreement.

Although the FLO supports efforts to establish bilateral and de facto agreements with all countries, the FLO's Thompson says it is the post itself that must take the lead on negotiating an agreement with the foreign ministry of the host country. The FLO provides posts with all the necessary supporting documentation. The critical ingredients to successful completion of a bilateral work agreement are post commitment and host country willingness. Some agreements take years to become final, and negotiations can be knocked off course by changes in host-country governments or by departure from post of whoever was taking the lead on the issue.

Spouses at posts in countries without bilateral agreements complain about lack of concern from post management. It is often the Community Liaison Officer who takes the lead on negotiating a bilateral, but without support from the front office, the CLO—who does not hold an official diplomatic position—is unlikely to succeed. Many FS employees and spouses point out that a strong and clear mandate from Washington could encourage, or force, post leadership in countries where there either is no agreement, or where there is a faulty one, to put it higher on the agenda.

Complicating this issue is the fact that in many countries that do have an agreement in place, there are few local economy jobs available to spouses, and those that are available are often at pay far below U.S. standards. In addition, some of the official agreements that are in place do not function effectively, while in some countries where no agreement is in place, FS spouses are able to work outside the Embassy anyway.

Best-Bet Professions

Having a career while serving as a Foreign Service spouse depends on attitude, flexibility, transportable skills, strategic bidding, and luck. There are certain professions that do lend themselves to the mobile and not always predictable FS lifestyle. A basic list (not in rank order) might read like this: teaching, training, translating/interpreting, writing/editing, Web design, website management, information technology, consulting and project management, public health, accounting and finance, law, art, freelancing, and home-based businesses.

There are, of course, many caveats that go with each type of occupation on the list. For example, there are teaching jobs all over the world, but salaries are low. Wendy Schmitz, a certified K-8 teacher and FS spouse, said, "When my husband joined the Foreign Service, we were told I would not have a problem finding work. To date this has been true. What everyone failed to tell us was that I would be on a different salary tier than my 'international hire' counterparts with the same qualifications." The FLO's Thompson confirms that teaching is one of the most portable and marketable professions, but poor salaries and extremely limited benefits are consistent problems for educators.

Attorney spouses have mixed experiences finding employment overseas, and much depends on the kind of law they practice and the specific country situation. Lawyer Steve Payne, married to a former USAID lawyer and now practicing in Washington, told us "There are opportunities for lawyers in civil society, democracy, legal reform and human rights programs in many countries. The work is most suitable for lawyers with litigation experience. In more commercial places, such as Indonesia, there are also opportunities in corporate law." (Indonesia is not one of the countries with a work agreement in place, but that has not stopped many spouses from working outside the mission there.)

Writers don't usually make a lot of money, but writing can be a rewarding profession that is highly portable. Some of the FS spouses who seem most at peace with Foreign Service life are the writers. Francesca Kelly told us that "Nowadays, being overseas, especially in a posting with reliable Internet connections, is perfect for a writer—you can't help having all these incredible experiences that you want to put on paper, and even the bad days are fodder for essays and articles." Kelly, along with Fritz Galt, was the founder of the *Spouses Underground Newsletter*, the SUN, which served to support and connect spouses and give a forum for satire and humor. It evolved into the *Tales from a Small Planet* website (**www.talesmag.com**), which has a broader scope.

The field of public health can offer a highly flexible career path for the FS spouse, offering employment or consulting options with international organizations, USAID or USAID contracting organizations, and with nonprofit organizations. Public health professionals with expertise in traditional international health areas such as child survival, maternal health and family planning have done well in developing countries, but find that jobs in more-developed countries are scarce. Technical skills in health education, epidemiology, needs-assessment, and program design are in demand in many developing countries.

According to the FLO's Thompson, more spouses are finding ways to take their jobs with them when they go overseas, arranging contracts with their home-base employers for work that can be done remotely via the Internet. Even some spouses working for the federal government have found success with this approach.

Language barriers to good jobs on the local economy can be significant for many spouses who were unable to study the language of the country before arriving at post. Although the Foreign Service Institute tries to include spouses in language classes, many spouses are unable to study while still in the U.S. either because of a lack of space in a class or for financial and other reasons. Many if not most spouses find themselves in-country before beginning study of the local language. In certain parts of the world the spouse without the local language will have an extremely difficult time finding a job on the local economy. This problem seems to be most acute in countries where Spanish or French are spoken.

Jobs in the Mission

Mission employment is an option for FS spouses in many posts around the world, though these positions are, more often than not, "support" jobs and come with artificially low salaries. Paula Riddle, FLO's employment program coordinator until recently, told AAFSW in an interview that "We are painfully aware of low salaries and are currently addressing this in our active working group. The EFM positions were classified a number of years ago and we feel that many need to be reclassified."

Many spouses feel underappreciated and underpaid in their mission jobs. FSO Roger Street put it bluntly, "The department more or less takes this deep and diverse pool of talent for granted, tapping into it at the department's pleasure and assuming that these folks will take anything that is offered."

Many spouses working inside U.S. missions work on Personal Service Contracts (PSCs) in positions that come with no benefits and that are not considered long-term positions. Others work as PITS (part-time, intermittent or temporary appointments), who are eligible for only limited benefits.

The good news is that many mission jobs are now being designated Family Member Appointments (FMA) as part of a program that started in 1998. Some FMAs fill FSO slots in short-staffed consular sections. FMAs are eligible for full benefits including annual leave and retirement. These benefits accrue with each subsequent FMA job. The FLO's employment data from 150 participating posts in 1999 showed that of family members working inside U.S. missions, 39 percent were on PSCs, 34 percent were in FMA positions, 18 percent were in PIT positions, and nine percent were working for mission recreation associations. However, spouses are worried that with the major increase in hiring currently underway at State and USAID, FMA jobs may become scarcer as junior officers retake some of those positions.

What Is Being Done?

What is being done for the FS spouse who wants to have a career, including employment with each posting? A lot but, perhaps, still not enough.

State management finally seems to realize that there is a connection between "recruitment and retention"—priority issues for the Foreign Service under Secretary Powell—and spousal employment opportunities. This appears to be leading to increased attention to spousal employment. However, as the FLO's Thompson puts it, "there is no silver bullet."

There are many spouses and FS employees who complain that State management has not done enough on the spousal employment front and has never made it a top priority. One FS spouse, who declined to be named, expressed dismay at the lack of interest she still sees from State: "State views spouse employment as something to work on after everything else is done, which is never."

To be fair, the FLO and the others tasked with working on this issue have a daunting task. Each host country has different issues influencing work opportunities. Each FS spouse is also unique, with his or her own priorities, goals, skills, and employment interests. FLO's efforts on the spousal employment front have expanded in recent years, and more information and assistance for FS spouses is becoming available, especially via e-mail and the Web.

The FLO's Mexico Spouse Assistance pilot program, known as MESA, was established in Mexico City, Monterrey and Guadalajara in 2000 to assist FS spouses seeking local economy employment in their professional fields. The assistance, according to the FLO, "is in the form of culturally specific job search tips and techniques along with an established network of professional contacts." The MESA program has not received rave reviews, however, in part because some family members mistakenly thought it was a job placement service rather than the less ambitious employment assistance program it was.

The pilot program has been expanded into a new program called SNAP, the Spouse Networking Assistance Program, and is being extended to include London, Brussels, Warsaw, Krakow, Tokyo, Seoul, Singapore, Cairo, Buenos Aires and Santiago. There is interest from State management in making it work, and the program has received significant funding for the expansion. Representatives from the FLO will visit each participating post this coming summer to check on the status of program implementation.

State management has also formed a Family Member Employment Working Group made up of employee relations personnel from the FLO and related human resources offices. The group meets weekly to discuss spousal employment issues and the policies that impact on spouse employment. According to Thompson, the group has come up with new ideas and solutions to problems, and has encouraged more open communication about the issue.

There are currently 162 posts participating in the FLO's Family Member Employment Report program. The FAMER database is a collection of information about local employment options from posts around the world. It lists current vacancies as well as lists positions held by family members inside and outside the mission. Data are collected by each participating post's CLO. The database can be accessed via State's Intranet site (http://hrweb.hr.state.gov/flo), but not via the Internet.

The FLO also publishes family member employment-related newsletters, now available by e-mail. The "Global Employment Monthly" is published monthly for family members seeking jobs overseas. "Network" is published twice monthly and is for family members seeking employment in the Washington, D.C. area. (Subscribe to the GEM at **www.state.gov/m/dghr/flo/7236.htm**. To subscribe to "Network," replace 7236 with 7237.) Family members can find more employment information on the FLO website, and can link to related FLO publications from the page: **www.stat.gov/m/dghr/flo/c1959.htm**. FLO welcomes employment questions from family members via phone: (202) 647–1076, or e-mail: **flo@state.gov**.

A Final Reality Check

Employment for FS family members has become an increasingly critical issue for recruiting and retaining FS employees as the dynamics of American society have changed over the last several decades and more and more families are two-career households. However, State and the other FS agencies will never be able to ensure every spouse will have the kind of work he or she is seeking.

As was true in 1957, the nature of the Foreign Service career still dictates that not only the FS employee, but the whole family accompanying him or her, represents the U.S. abroad. It may never be possible for the FS spouse's career to take top billing in a Foreign Service family. But what has changed since 1957 is the notion that a FS spouse cannot have a separate and meaningful career of his or her own. The real trick now is figuring out how to make it work.

This article originally appeared in the Foreign Service Journal, *May 2002.*

Work Options for Spouses Abroad

by Patricia Linderman

Accompanying a Foreign Service Officer or other government employee overseas doesn't just mean a change in location—it is a major change in lifestyle, including your career opportunities. Abroad, you will face barriers to your professional ambitions that would never have existed at home, from work permit restrictions to shockingly low local pay scales.

The good news is that more work opportunities exist for accompanying spouses than ever before. The bad news is that they are still very limited, and you will have to be proactive—and sometimes creative—to carve out a professional niche for yourself as a Foreign Service spouse. This essay will cover some of the options you might consider, as well as some strategies for deciding which one(s) are right for you.

Option 1: Taking a Job in the Embassy or Consulate

Besides the jobs filled by Foreign Service Officers and specialists and by host-country employees (called Foreign Service Nationals or FSNs), most embassies have a number of jobs which are offered to accompanying spouses.

These may include the Community Liaison Office coordinator (CLO), who helps support the American officers and their families; secretaries and assistants to various officers; visa examiners and other positions in the Consular Section; and the Embassy nurse. The jobs may be part-time or full-time. Other agencies represented at post may also offer positions. In addition, spouses may also be hired on a contract basis for special projects, such as editing the post newsletter or conducting a cost-of-living survey.

On the plus side, these jobs are, by definition, in the same location as your partner's assignment. They also give you immediate involvement in the interesting daily work of an Embassy overseas. Even if you are "just" the assistant to the personnel officer, you will have a security clearance, wear a badge, and probably be treated with great respect by the local employees. This can be an important boost to your self-esteem when you are newly-arrived in a strange country, struggling with simple tasks like shopping for food, and wondering what you have gotten yourself into.

Spouses who feel that they need some sort of work for their own personal equilibrium, and who are not so concerned with staying in a specific professional field, are often quite satisfied with these jobs. For spouses interested in making a career in this way, there is a "professional associates" program that helps provide employment continuity and maintains their security clearance between posts.

On the negative side, these jobs (called "PIT" jobs, for "part-time, intermittent or temporary") are mostly low-level and low-paid. Spouses come and go every few years, and Embassy management cannot count on getting highly-skilled or experienced replacements, so the jobs are basically aimed at a lowest-common-denominator level. In fact, some spouses complain that they are considered a "captive labor pool," expected to do work no one else wants to do for little compensation.

However, as many skilled spouses choose to work independently or not to work at all rather than take a low-paid PIT job, it is possible that salaries may inch upward as an incentive. Also, some unfilled Foreign Service Officer jobs have recently been offered to qualified spouses, in an effort to make greater use of the talent pool we represent. Finally, it sometimes happens that temporary jobs are created at post for spouses with special talents. For instance, a (male) spouse who was an architect was hired to help oversee the major renovation of the U.S. Interests Section in Havana, Cuba. Consider communicating with the administrative section of your assigned post in advance to see if there is some way to put your professional skills to mutually advantageous use.

Option 2: Working for Another Organization

Foreign Service spouses have found satisfying work with international schools, language institutes, multinational companies, nonprofit organizations, development agencies, universities, and many other American, international or local organizations.

One advantage you may offer to international organizations is that you are already in the country—your employer does not have to pay for your move or give you a housing allowance. On the other hand, you may be offered a lower compensation package for the same reason—that "captive labor pool" problem again. It is often a good idea to line up this kind of job before you arrive at post, so that you are considered an expatriate rather than a "local hire." Getting up a work permit may be more difficult after you arrive, as well.

One source of frustration in this sort of career is your dependence on your partner's schedule. Foreign Service assignments last some two to four years at most, and then you face starting all over again in a new country (although if you are lucky, you can bid on places where your organization has branch offices). Furthermore, assignments are sometimes canceled at the last minute, for instance when a position is suddenly abolished. And as an accompanying spouse, you may have no authorization to live in the country before your spouse arrives or after he or she leaves.

As usual, you may have to strike a balance between satisfying work, time spent between jobs, and periods of separation—or a very long "commute," as with one spouse who teaches at a university in Austria while his wife is posted at a Consulate in Germany.

International schools are the employer of choice for many Foreign Service spouses, since they are found in nearly all capital cities around the world and generally offer one-year work contracts. A special program in the Washington area is offered to help spouses earn teacher certification in one year before going abroad: FAST-TRAIN (Foreign Affairs Spouses Teacher Training Project), at George Mason University.

For work on the local economy, conditions vary widely from country to country. Work permits may be easy, difficult or impossible to obtain, depending on the country. Local salary levels may be attractive—or, more often, seem practically insulting. Proficiency in the local language may be required for most jobs. There may also be bureaucratic barriers and/or high local tax levels.

Still, if things work out right, a local job can be a great way to meet interesting people in your host country and deepen your overseas experience. Some spouses, faced with work restrictions and low salaries, even decide to volunteer their time instead of being paid, to gain the experience without the hassles (and with the flexibility of being a volunteer).

No matter what kind of outside work you seek, you are expected to get permission from the Ambassador or chief of mission at post. This is to ensure that your work is compatible with the diplomatic work of the mission; after all, you are there on a diplomatic passport and visa. For example, working for a political lobbying firm would obviously be frowned upon. Check before you accept a job—it's true that some spouses rely on a "don't ask, don't tell" policy, but potential consequences could include being kicked out of the country with your unhappy diplomatic partner.

Option 3: Freelancing or Telecommuting

The advent of the Internet has made freelancing and telecommuting a much more attractive option for Foreign Service spouses. With a home computer system and reliable Internet connection (now available in most countries), you can work for clients in the United States and around the world.

If you are leaving an enjoyable job behind in the United States, consider the possibility of telecommuting or working on contract for your former employer. You may be surprised at the range of tasks you can still accomplish from abroad. For instance, you may be able to design training programs, write manuals or do consulting by e-mail.

The pluses of independent work include the satisfaction, pay and respect that comes from a job, combined with more flexibility for family, travel and personal time. Starting your own business can give you a chance to use your creativity, be your own boss and perhaps try something new.

Also, if you are working over the Internet, a laptop and Web-based e-mail address lets you take your work with you each time you move and not have to start all over again—a very important benefit for people who change countries every few years!

Potential negatives of freelance work include social isolation, the administrative hassles of running your own business, uncertain pay, and the need for a lot of personal initiative.

Writing in all its forms can be a very portable and satisfying career for Foreign Service spouses: consider creative writing, travel journalism, translating, copyediting, technical writing, nonfiction writing, or whatever field interests you. The Internet itself is also a source of many opportunities, such as website design and web editing.

However, not every freelance career is Internet-based, of course; many spouses find customers at post (usually other Americans or third-country expatriates) for services such as hairstyling, catering, party planning, personal organizing, computer troubleshooting, fitness coaching, etc.

Teaching and training are areas of great opportunity for freelancers: the possibilities include teaching English, tutoring students, giving music lessons, teaching specialty cooking courses, or giving seminars or workshops. Or use your experience in more than one culture to become a cross-cultural consultant or trainer—large companies and local relocation firms often hire people on contract for this kind of work.

Of course, since you are in the country on a diplomatic visa and probably living in government housing, your freelance business won't be as "free" as it would be at home. According to State Department regulations, spouses' home businesses must be approved by the ambassador or chief of mission and must not violate local laws or harm the interests of the diplomatic mission—as interpreted by post management. Clearly, you aren't going to be allowed to breed dogs in government housing, or to have hundreds of clients coming to your door in a residential area. Even seemingly harmless work may be seen as "undiplomatic," such as writing travel articles for a newspaper that regularly criticizes the host government.

The use of the mail system is another sore point—you may not use the diplomatic pouch or APO mail for business purposes. You certainly can't order products such as Tupperware or Amway through the pouch or APO system for resale to clients, and you are not even supposed to order supplies for your business that way, such as hairstyling equipment or even professional books! Since many countries do not have a reliable local mail system as an alternative, this can be a real hardship. Ways to get around it include anticipating your needs and including supplies in your household shipment; using international express mail services; asking visitors to bring you books and supplies; or simply keeping your mail use very modest and unobtrusive, so you don't attract negative attention.

Getting a local work permit and/or paying local taxes for a small home business is another gray area. If your clients are all fellow diplomatic passport holders, or located in other countries (via Internet), this should not be a problem. The more local clients you have, however, the more likely you will attract attention and need to go through the formal paperwork to register your business.

Option 4: Becoming a Tandem Couple

One sure way to find employment abroad is to join the Foreign Service yourself, if you qualify and are interested. According to 2001 statistics, 11% of officers are members of a "tandem couple."

The pluses of this choice include a professional job and salary. Efforts are made to find both of you jobs at the same Embassy or Consulate, although this obviously limits your choices. Neither of you can supervise the other, of course, but it is usually no problem to juggle the management chain to avoid this.

Like everyone else, tandem couples must sometimes make work/life compromises. For instance, if one partner is offered a career-enhancing assignment at a place with no job for the other partner, they weigh the options of turning down the assignment, working in two different countries, or having the other partner come along to the career-enhancing post on "leave without pay" (LWOP) status.

Taking up a career with a related foreign affairs agency, such as USAID, can be another "tandem" option, although in this case, the opportunities for assignments together may be even more limited.

Option 5: Thinking Outside the (Work) Box

You may have been employed all your adult life and have trouble imagining not working. But for many Foreign Service spouses, an assignment abroad makes employment more difficult and other options more attractive.

With free housing, utilities and other allowances abroad, many couples find that they have an additional $15–20,000 per year in disposable income, making a second salary less necessary. Faced with the less-than-ideal job options abroad, many spouses choose instead to stay home with their children, do something creative (like take art lessons or write a novel), help others as a volunteer, pursue their favorite sport or hobby, or just enjoy exploring their host country.

At-home parenting in the Foreign Service can be especially satisfying for both mothers and fathers. There are usually international parents' groups for company, made up of people from a wide range of nationalities. Inexpensive household help in many countries lets you spend quality time with your children rather than worrying about the chores. Foreign Service kids often need extra support during an international move, which an at-home parent is well-placed to provide. And you can even consider the time you spend parenting your Foreign Service children as a contribution to world peace: aren't these multilingual young people, with their experience crossing cultures, exactly what our troubled planet needs?

Strategies

With all of the choices above, all with their own difficulties, how can you decide what work option is right for you, and then find it? There's no easy answer, but here are some suggestions:

Know thyself. Take stock of your education, work experience and interests before you go overseas. What are your most portable skills? Would you consider working independently? Is there something outside of work you've always wanted to do?

Keep your priorities straight. Working as a Foreign Service spouse usually involves compromises. You may find interesting work for a non-profit organization that hardly pays, or a great career opportunity that requires you to live in a different country from your spouse. What is most important to you: Interesting work? Making money? Developing your professional skills? Working part-time or at home? Avoiding long periods of separation? A job that fits your true priorities will give more satisfaction in the long run.

Build portable skills. Consider additional training to enhance your marketability overseas. Some functional, computer and language training courses are offered by the State Department to spouses on a space-available basis. Or take the initiative to strengthen your skills in a portable field such as web design, travel journalism or public health development.

Network, network, network. Outside of Embassy positions, most jobs and opportunities are found through networking, not advertisements. As soon as you know where you are going, make as many in-country contacts as possible (start with Foreign Service colleagues, online expatriate groups and organizations related to your profession) and ask for advice with your job search.

Keep tax implications in mind. If you are working in a PIT job for the U.S. government abroad, your income is subject to full U.S. taxes. Freelance work, however—including work on a contract basis for the Embassy—falls under the overseas income exemption (although you do have to pay self-employment tax). Working for a local or international company may make you liable for local taxes. These distinctions can have a significant effect on your final salary. Talk to your administrative office at post or an expatriate tax specialist for specific advice.

Have a Plan B. The unexpected happens everywhere, but especially in Foreign Service life. Your partner's assignment may be canceled, or you may be evacuated from post. The work permit for your dream job may never come through. Thinking through contingency plans in advance can help you through these kinds of crises.

Enjoy the adventure. As a Foreign Service spouse, you may not always have the most interesting job. But you'll certainly have an interesting **life**, as well as (if things go right) the time and flexibility to enjoy your host country. Make the most of it!

Foreign Service Families Ride the Information Superhighway

by Kelly Midura

La Paz was our first Foreign Service assignment.

Where?

I could not have told you the answer until we spent a weekend at the Arlington County Library, digging through stacks of travel books, bid list in hand.

Now we knew that La Paz is the capital of Bolivia, that the national currency was the *boliviano*, that one could visit Titicaca, the highest navigable lake in the world, and that the local women wore bowler hats and nine petticoats, but that was about it. The State Department's Overseas Briefing Center provided a few more clues as to what life might be like in this remote capital, but most of the information was sadly outdated. A single-page form letter was our sole communication with the post's Community Liaison Office Coordinator (CLO). As a result, we relied almost exclusively on the official State Department Post Report to bid on La Paz and to prepare for our first overseas transfer. This was in 1988 and 1989. How primitive that process seems now!

Our assignment to Bolivia turned out to be a positive experience, in part because as a couple in our early twenties who could easily fit our entire lives into a few suitcases, we could adapt to just about anything. Of course, it was a shock to me that there were no decent jobs whatsoever for English-speaking recent college graduates (this was not exactly how the Post Report had described the situation). But by the end of the tour, like many other Foreign Service wives, I had employed myself, at least temporarily, by getting pregnant.

A later tour to Zambia turned out to be a mistake for us. At our second post, Guatemala, we borrowed post reports from the Community Liaison Office, spread them out on the bed, and simply made the best guess possible of which of the available options would be the best place to take our new family. Alas, the description of Lusaka as a "clean and attractive city" must have dated from the 1950s. We were in no way prepared for what awaited us in that AIDS-ravaged country that was literally falling apart in front of our eyes.

Two kids, three continents, four cats, five tours, ten years, and several unmentionable diseases later, the bidding process had been radically altered by information technology.

When my husband presented me with his last list of options, in 1996, headed by a job in Prague, Czech Republic, my first thought was to go online. What's the school like? Type in "Prague and international school" and see the institution in full color. How's the weather? Go to Yahoo! Weather and find today's forecast along with seasonal average temperatures and rainfall. Want to see the city? Type in "Prague and photos" to see everything from online tourist brochures and Czech city sites to someone's Aunt Edna's photos of her last visit to Prague.

We made solid choices based on a wealth of information from a variety of sources, and as a result the entire family's stress level was lowered. You might think it would be pretty hard to lose with Europe, but every area of the world does have its special considerations for someone. I ruled out a nearby post based on winter temperatures that routinely dip to twenty degrees below zero. The point is that we researched the questions that were important to us, and found answers to them online.

Our experience is becoming more and more typical. The flip side of this free flow of information, of course, is that many hardship posts are now going begging for officers. While short staffing in the State

Department is certainly one reason for this, I suspect that it may also be because officers *and their family members* are now easily able to obtain unfiltered information about most countries. "Real Post Reports," travelogues, online journals, tourist sites, news sites, message boards and discussion lists such as AAFSW's Livelines have given us reams of information to weigh along with the information that the State Department chooses to provide. Consequently, many families are less willing to bid on some places than they might have been previous to the existence of the Information Superhighway.

After the assignment to Prague was offered and accepted, I was able to communicate quickly and directly with the CLO and with other spouses at post via email, rather than through the official cables and "tie line" phone calls that used to be the exclusive responsibility of the officer. Because my questions were asked and answered *directly*, there was far less miscommunication and frustration than there had been with previous assignments! My future neighbor even sent me digital photos of my new house via email. This last was particularly helpful for my children, who were far less concerned with castles and works of art than they were with the size of their new back yard and bedrooms. Simply knowing basic facts about the house, the school, the weather, and everything that would make up the mundane fabric of our new life was a godsend.

We had about as complete a picture of our new home as possible before arriving. Not only we were able to assimilate the myriad parts of our new life more smoothly but our sense of loss was lessened by not having to leave as much behind. Yes, there were painful goodbyes to both people and places. But within hours of my arrival in Prague I was in email contact with my family. The day after that I was emailing friends, and participating in the same online writers' group that I had joined two years before in Washington. Before long I was listening to National Public Radio via streaming audio, reading the Washington Post online, and shopping via Internet at Old Navy and The Gap. It feels as if a large part of my world has remained unchanged, despite the upheaval of an international move. The addition of a little stability and permanence into the ever-changing mix of this expatriate lifestyle has helped keep me sane.

We continue to stay in close contact with family and friends via the Internet, sharing our lives through a family home page, an online journal, scanned photos and children's artwork that we email home on a regular basis. Most recently, this flow of contact has expanded to include free voice chat service and cheap Internet phone calls. Three cents a minute! It was so hard to stay close to family less than a decade ago, when each phone call was marked by anxious glances at the hands of the clock. There were times during those long, lonely days in Africa when our phone bill exceeded two hundred dollars a month, a figure that we could ill afford on my husband's salary. Those days are no more, and I don't miss them a bit.

When my daughter was born in Guatemala in 1991 my husband rushed to have photos developed, then faxed them to my mother, who oohed and aahed over the gray blobs that came out of her fax machine in Nashville. This seemed remarkably advanced at the time. At the same daughter's tenth birthday party, I took digital photographs, plugged my camera into the computer and uploaded two dozen photos to an online developing service, then invited my mother and other relatives to view them in slide show format on the other side of the world. Not only were they able to experience my daughter's birthday party in living color just a few hours after the event, but they could order their own copies of the photos right away. (I think we'll buy a web cam before the next birthday and let everyone see her blowing out the candles in streaming video.)

While the numerous means of communication offered by the Internet have considerable emotional value, there are wonderful practical applications as well. The issue of spouse employment is one that has dogged the Foreign Service for years, with little, if any, improvement. Embassy jobs are often dead-end and poorly-paid, and local restrictions and wage scales still keep many spouses from finding meaningful, profitable careers.

But now we have alternatives. I am writing this essay from my home office in Prague, from which I manage websites owned by individuals and organizations all over the world. Several of these contracts were acquired prior to my arrival here, and all of them can be continued after I return to the United States. When I'm not busy working on websites, I write articles and essays for various travel and expatriate publications that I query and submit via email. Many Foreign Service spouses employed as writers, editors, researchers and consultants of all types have taken advantage of the fast and direct communication made possible by the Internet. If you can telecommute, you can do it from anywhere.

Now here's the really great part, more important than keeping myself occupied or earning a decent wage: my career is largely independent of the Embassy, my husband's plans, and the whims of the State Department. I do not have to wait for a security clearance, deal with changes in Embassy administration and policy, or navigate the same office politics that my husband does. I do not have to worry about losing my job, or taking a salary cut when he is transferred, as long as I make sure that we end up in a country with Internet service and a bilateral work agreement. Kelly's Web Studio is *mine* and mine alone, as are its successes and failures. This is one area of my life in which I am not a "spouse/dependent." And isn't that, after all, what today's Foreign Service partners really want?

Some point to the Internet as a sign of people's alienation from each other. They say that email is no substitute for conversation: that the Internet causes us to withdraw from our fellow human beings. I have found that, at least in the microcosm of the Foreign Service, the opposite is the case. The Internet can strengthen friendships and family ties that might be hard to maintain otherwise. Conversations can be started online and continued online for years, often leading to "real-world" friendships. Through email discussion groups and message boards, like-minded people can meet and support each other personally and professionally through life-altering events such as packouts. "Trailing" spouses can develop professionally across time zones and transfers with minimal disruption. Goodbyes are a little easier when the lines of communication are so easy to maintain.

Cyberspace is no substitute for the real world, but it can certainly add a dimension that may be lacking in some parts of that world. While our lives as partners of diplomats will never be easy, communication technology has changed our world in ways that we never could have anticipated a mere decade ago. For this Foreign Service family, the world seems a smaller and friendlier place as a result.

Tips for Non-Technophiles

by Pat Olsen

1. Find a tech-savvy friend to be your computer mentor. In fact, find two. A friend at post will help you with the glitches and complications of your computer, software and associated gadgets such as printer and scanner. Your adviser in the U.S. will keep you informed about what's new, tell you what to get and when to wait. Be prepared to do whatever is necessary to cultivate these friends. Bribe them with cookies, wine, chocolate; watch the kids, walk the dog. Your efforts will be repaid when your friend rescues you from the inevitable panic that comes with a contrary computer.

2. The computer question of today is: One or two? Laptop or desktop? Many families are finding that two computers are a necessity. Adult family members don't want to juggle computer usage between two schedules, and the kids need daily computer time for schoolwork.

Laptops match our mobile lifestyle. Computers have become so essential that we can no longer do without them for the months between packing out and receiving household effects at our onward assignment. Managing the myriad details requiring attention during home leave or training without access to your computer is a most unpleasant thought. A laptop allows us to take everything with us, on a moment's notice if necessary.

3. Be sure you have a high-speed modem installed to maximize your online access capability. If you have two computers in the family, buy splitters that allow more than one phone cord to connect into one line and several lengths of phone cords so each computer can connect.

4. With a digital camera, you can send pictures back to family without the hassles of film and developing, both of which can be problematic when overseas. Take as many pictures as you want, keep only the best, and send them to friends around the world the same day. Your host country friends may well be your biggest photo fans, delighting in e-mailed pictures of the picnic you shared together.

Digital cameras are surprisingly easy to use. Consult the manual and camera-expert friends. Buy a battery charger and re-chargeable batteries for your camera, and an extra memory card. Soon, with some simple tech know-how, you can change your screen-saver to a scrolling photo show of your latest adventures.

5. A scanner is even handier overseas than in the United States. When the reliability of mail delivery is in doubt, the ability to convert documents to images to send between computers is very useful. It also doubles as a photocopier, handy for on-the-spot needs.

6. If your computer doesn't already have one, purchase a CD-RW drive. It enables you to back-up your hard drive to a CD, as well as to save your digital photos to a CD instead of using up computer memory with photo files. Send your family all the fabulous pictures from your last exotic vacation. No more boxes of unfiled photos, loose negatives or worries about dampness control.

7. Do you need to be convinced about the benefits of owning a hand-held? After packing out, waving husband off, wandering among the homes of assorted relatives and friends for six weeks, and finally dropping youngest child at college, this frazzled veteran spouse made a desperate, spur-of-the-moment-purchase of a hand-held. After loading in list after list, addresses, phone numbers, passwords, pins, reminders, driving directions and calendar dates, she threw a million bits of paper to the wind and is living happily ever after. Synchronization of your hand-held with your computer means the same information is available on the road or at the desk. On a short trip or long, the information you

need in an emergency is with you, as well as a calculator for currency exchanges, city and time zone information and an alarm. Advanced users can use a hand-held to access e-mail and the Internet.

8. Once you're equipped, you arrive at post, find a local server and set up your local e-mail account. How many times has your e-mail address changed? You can "be someone.com" by registering your own domain name. The author, for example, is **pat@olsenglobal.com**. First, go to an online domain name registration site, easily found through a search engine. Check to see what name combinations have already been used and create an original .com name for yourself. In our case, olsen.com was already registered, so we created olsenglobal.com. Register the domain name you have chosen for $35 per year. This gives you a permanent e-mail address as well as a World Wide Web address to use for your own web page.

To use your new .com address, sign up with an Internet provider who will be your home "post office" and receive mail for your .com address. You then arrange to have your mail forwarded to your local overseas Internet provider through whom you can pick up your mail at post via a local online connection. When you go on temporary duty (TDY) or home leave, or depart post, all you do is contact your domain name server to change your forwarding address to receive your mail at a new location. In addition, your server may offer means to access your main account to check mail while you're away, thereby avoiding the need to use a forwarding address for short trips. Your correspondents will continue to use your same .com address no matter where you move. Give family members their own individual addresses at your .com domain name and each can have mail forwarded to his own address. College kids who use a family domain name have their mail forwarded to college during the year, redirect it to post or home for the summer and redirect it again when they return to school. The kids like this because their mail won't show up in Mom's or Dad's mailbox, but in their own. The low cost for a family domain name with a secure, individually controlled, permanent e-mail address more than pays for itself for those with a transient lifestyle. Accounts such as Hotmail, Yahoo and AOL provide similar e-mail accessibility, if you don't mind being a member of a large group and relying on the organization's stability.

9. Before you go overseas, have your choice of software installed or updated, and bring a couple of basic reference books and documentation for all your equipment. Begin to use a new program or new equipment before you leave so you won't have problems when you arrive at post. (See bribing stateside friend, #1.) The U.S. government anti-virus programs are by license available to home users. Take advantage and install virus protection, and keep it updated with downloads. Don't go overboard buying software for your children. Wait to see what the school recommends. No matter how small or isolated the post, your kids can find activities beyond just computers and videos.

10. Go into an office supply store and treat yourself to all sorts of neat stuff that will come in useful overseas. Buy printable blanks for address labels, business cards, stationery and notecards; a variety of photo and novelty photo paper; printing paper in a selection of weights and colors, from neon to elegant. Buy extra ink cartridges, CDs, diskettes—anything you might need in the middle of the night and don't want to wait for, even though computer supplies are increasingly available even in remote locations.

Keep in mind, however, that the size of U.S. paper and filing supplies differs from much of the rest of the world. Printers adjust to a variety of paper sizes but your filing system won't. Use U.S. paper with U.S. notebooks, file folders, sheet protectors and a three-hole punch. European A-4 paper is longer and narrower, requiring its own A-4 notebooks and folders, and a two-hole punch. Stock up on what you need. You may not want to buy the kids large quantities of U.S.-size notebooks and paper for school, but instead buy local supplies at post.

11. Technology moves at a rapid pace. Don't worry about being one or two steps behind. Just keep returning to Tip #1.

A Career in Diplomatic Security

by John Hampson

I am a Supervisory Special Agent and have been with the Diplomatic Security Service (DSS) for the past ten years. I love my career and am very proud to be a member of both DSS and the Foreign Service. I love my career because I have had so many opportunities to do what I want—visit many out of the way places around the world that I would never visit in a regular 9-to-5 position. I have seen and experienced some of the most exciting things and historical events, and have met extraordinary people—stuff most people only dream about or glimpse on CNN.

Overseas, as a Regional Security Officer (RSO), you are responsible for million-dollar guard programs, sometimes small armies of guards (at one time there were 400 local guards at our Embassy in Somalia, for example). You are in charge of molding that force into the best guard force it can be.

You are an investigator—working criminal, personal, and other more sensitive cases for DSS, and any, repeat, any U.S. law enforcement agency that asks for your help. You are the U.S. law enforcement representative for the U.S. government in many countries (approximately 200 postings worldwide)—especially where there is no FBI legatt (they are posted only in the Londons and Parises of the world). You work passport and visa criminal cases, child kidnapping cases, wanted criminal cases, and internal investigations of our employees (stressful, yes, but very necessary). You work murder cases, theft, etc.

Do you know what agency located and arrested Ramsi Youseff, the 1993 World Trade Center bomber—yes, DSS! Don't let anyone tell you it was the FBI. Watch it on an "America's Most Wanted" rerun. Without saying too much—you work counterintelligence cases, internal affairs, and soon computer forensic evidence cases. If you are an investigator type, the sky is the limit in DSS.

Overseas, you are a liaison officer between American businesses and the country councils that are set up at each post to advise them on local and international security issues. You also liaise with local police and military—a great way to develop lasting relationships for the U.S. government in law enforcement.

Again, overseas you are also responsible for all physical security at the Embassy. As a civilian, you have operational control and supervision over the U.S. Marine Corps detachment at your Embassy. Where else would a civilian supervise between five and thirty U.S. Marines? The only other people I know who do this are the Ambassador, the Secretary of Defense, and the Secretary of the Navy. Oh—I forgot the President!

I usually refer to the RSO as the "sheriff" of the Embassy. How accurately? Who knows.

There are many other responsibilities and benefits of working overseas as an RSO. A few examples in my case: meeting several U.S. presidents, all the secretaries of State, numerous congressmen and senators, other countries' presidents and foreign ministers, and even Ambassador Shirley Temple Black! I was the only American (besides the U.S. Marine Corps flight crew) to fly with Chairman Arafat to Camp David on Helo 1 a few years ago.

You are responsible for protecting all American employees at your post, including the Ambassador. For those of us who really care, this is a very important burden we as RSOs carry. I take it very seriously. We are also responsible for protecting the secrets of our nation—not something to take lightly, either.

Domestically, you could work on a counterterrorist / assault SWAT-type team (MSD) and travel with the Secretary of State or to threatened U.S. Embassies. You could be an instructor at the DS Training Center (my current position).

You could teach overseas at one of our three International Law Enforcement Academies (ILEA), in Budapest, Bangkok or Gaborone, funded and managed by the State Department's INL Bureau. You could be an Agent-in-Charge of a protective security detail (same as what the Secret Service does, both domestic and overseas). You could work criminal cases anywhere in the USA, hunting wanted terrorists and/or fugitives (I did this for three years, covering northern and western Virginia). I traveled as far as California and Colorado to arrest fugitives, document vendors, drug dealers, etc. I have testified in court, managed confidential informants, and spent many hours on surveillance. My agents located three missing children for the National Center for Missing and Exploited Children in Alexandria, Virginia.

In my last position, I supervised 19 of the best criminal investigators at the Washington Field Office. (DS has 22 field offices throughout the U.S., most in major cities.) You hopefully will never have to go to anything like the WTC recovery site in New York City, as I did for twelve days in September 2001. Probably the saddest time of my life. A team of 12 DSS agents from Washington DC, plus our New York agents, worked tirelessly for twelve days doing every job conceivable in support of recovering those missing in the WTC disaster.

Training is available—probably some of the best offered. Outside education is not often suggested but is available (I earned an M.S. degree that was paid for by DSS). I also had one year of Russian language at the Foreign Service Institute (I consider this a scholarship) and other excellent training.

Now the down side of the job. It is not for a person who wants all his or her weekends and nights free. This job can be tough on families.

According to the assignment you are in, hours can be demanding. As time goes on in your career, your schedule becomes more manageable, but the hours are still long. I have been married 13 years and so far have missed half my wife's birthdays, our anniversaries and Valentine's Days. I missed my son's birthday for two consecutive years. One summer, I spent five weeks in Uganda (sent on four days' notice). I was pulled for a two-month temporary duty (TDY) tour to Belgrade, Serbia last year to cover for the RSO (no post goes vacant when an RSO is traveling). The list goes on…

There are dangers—you are highly trained to carry firearms and are expected to use them when necessary. I have been in several dangerous incidents I would rather not discuss here. I can tell you I was in Moscow during the second coup. My family slept in the gym for two nights, while I was working. I have been in other serious events as well.

Without going into detail—you will be compensated very well for a government employee—count on your overtime plus your Law Enforcement Availability Pay (LEAP). Contrary to what colleagues may say, you will earn it—I am working on average ten-hour days to earn my LEAP and I am an upper/mid-level supervisor. Remember DSS agents are specialists, not Foreign Service Officers, so we are authorized overtime.

This is a very touchy subject in the Foreign Service, for the FSOs also work very long/hard hours and go uncompensated for their extra efforts. However, FSOs are commissioned by Congress, DSS agents are not.

Don't expect to become an ambassador working in DS; it is a rarity, although several of our senior DSS agents have been ambassadors. Currently, our Assistant Secretary for Security is designated as an ambassador. I believe we still have one DSS agent I know of who is currently an ambassador in Africa.

I could probably continue, but I believe I have hit the highlights and tried to give you a balanced view of some of the pros and cons of a career in DSS. It is probably slated toward the positive, but I am a positive thinker and this has helped me throughout my career. Remember, it is not a career for everyone. The best information I can give you is that DSS agents have career choices and they can make their career what they want it to be (no, this is not an Army advertisement!).

A final note—this past Christmas, I knew DSS had come a long way from the old days of being known as "SY" to a full-fledged security and law enforcement agency when I was walking through the toy aisle at Target in Alexandria and spotted the DSS Special Agent (GI Joe-style) action figure. Of course my little 8-year-old boy saw it and said "Daddy—this is you!" I only wish I had the physique of that doll!

PART VI
Moments of Crisis

After the Nairobi Bombing

An interview with Foreign Service spouse Joanne Grady-Huskey

Q: You are a survivor of the bombing of the American Embassy in Nairobi. Can you tell us about that day?

It was an ordinary day in Nairobi, Kenya. I had to take my children, Chris, age 8, and Caroline, age 5, to the Embassy doctor for their school physicals and then we planned to have lunch with my husband in the Embassy café. The doctor's office was in the basement of the Embassy, which was in a bad section of Nairobi. That day, I arrived and noticed the guard was acting a bit odd; while normally kind and friendly, he now seemed tense and anxious. Little did I know that I had parked next to a truck that had entered the Embassy grounds, and that the truck had a bomb in it. I proceeded with my children into the basement of the Embassy and on into the doctor's office.

Within about two minutes of our arrival, the entire place blew up and we were all thrown to the floor. I had to scramble to find my children in the rubble and dark confusion. Amazingly, we were all unharmed, but that wasn't true for a lot of other people. We gathered together in the dark cement dust and tried to figure out what had happened and where we were. We then climbed through the debris and cement out of the office, down the long corridor full of rubble, listening to the sounds of people calling out in pain.

We couldn't find an opening to get out, but finally found a light and climbed through a hole that led us into the garage where there was a wall of fire. We worked our way up a ramp to find that where our car had been was the epicenter of the bomb; the car was incinerated, and the city was in turmoil—buildings were down, people were wounded. Confusion and horror was all around us.

We ran around to the front of the Embassy, and my husband, who had been on the fourth floor of the Embassy in the Ambassador's office when the blast hit, came running around the perimeter of the Embassy at the exact same moment, to find us trapped inside the gates. He helped us escape and we all ran down the street away from the horror. My husband went back to help other victims, and we made our way home covered in black soot. The weeks and months that followed were some of the most difficult of our lives. Many people we knew had been killed. Many people were wounded either physically or emotionally. The sorrow was overwhelming. Everyone in the Embassy community began to work to put the Embassy and our lives back together. The community pulled together in the aftermath to rebuild and regroup. The individual efforts of so many people, both American and Kenyan, who valiantly worked to prove that the terrorists could not win, helped to heal the collective wounds of our trauma. But still it has taken years to heal.

Q: Did anything prepare you for such a devastating event? Did you receive any kind of training before going overseas?

I took the Security Overseas Seminar (SOS) course at the Foreign Service Institute before I moved overseas. That course is now required for all employees and is recommended for family members. It covers all the possible traumas that could occur while you are in the Foreign Service. The course is useful; a bit frightening, but certainly a must. It is terribly important to get that kind of information in today's world. We also were briefed by the Regional Security Office in Nairobi when we first arrived about the dangers of living in Nairobi.

They covered theft, carjacking, and other forms of violent acts, but no one predicted a terrorist bomb in Kenya, so although we were on the alert for crime, the bombing was a shock. Today people will be more prepared for that eventuality, since almost all security training will cover bomb threats.

Q: What about the practical aspects of dealing with terrorism? Is there anything people can do to prepare themselves (without being paranoid about it)?

People now realize after September 11 that Americans are targets anywhere in the world. There is no longer safety from terrorism even in our own country. When overseas, the best advice is to avoid doing anything in public places that identifies you as an American. Keep a very low profile; watch how you dress and speak. Follow all the rules of precaution, such as checking cars before you enter, not displaying American flags on your luggage, etc., not accepting packages, not loitering in open lobbies or public areas, and keeping your U.S. passport and your name and address concealed.

The SOS course and Regional Security Office briefings at post go over these specifics and many others in great detail. It is vital to be informed about the country you are going to and about the political status and the risk of threat. The more informed you are, the less likely you will be caught off guard in the event of an attack. Be sure that your children are also informed.

Q: What about families with children? Are there any specific considerations to be aware of?

People with children have to be aware that the children also can be targets. It is important to check the security of your home—the alarm system, the fire escapes, the guards. It is also important to check the security and emergency plans for the American or international school that your children attend. This includes the security procedures in place for the school bus as well.

It is advisable to have a contingency plan in place for your family in the event of an attack. Discuss with your children what to do if they are in a bombing, carjacking, kidnapping, etc. Talk through with them how they can feel safe, how they can contact you, and what your family will do to be safe. It is important not to scare them, but to reassure them that systems are in place and provide them with the knowledge of how to proceed in the safest, calmest manner.

Q: After the bombing, you had a choice to be evacuated, yet you opted to stay in Kenya. Why?

Our family and almost all of the families who were in the bombing in Nairobi opted to stay on in Kenya, even though we were offered immediate evacuation. Most of us felt that it was important for us and our families to maintain normal life as much as possible. Our children were about to start school, in a school they had attended for two years. They had their friends, their routines, their after-school activities. We felt, as did others, that it was best not to upset our homes and move at this time of trauma, but to try to get life back to normal as quickly as possible.

Also, it was so useful to be in the same place as others who had gone through the bombing. We needed to talk about it, to console each other, to respond individually and as a community to the trauma. It is healing to be able to help. We all did our part to get things back to normal. As Chair of the American Women's Association, I was able to set up a relief fund for Kenyan victims, and to fund the rehabilitation of several people who were severely wounded in the blast. The interaction with Kenyan victims of the bombing was healing for me as well as for them. We were able to share our sorrow, and react in a constructive way to the devastation. The U.S. government also was extremely involved in helping Kenyans who were injured by the bombing. Had we not had this opportunity, much more misunderstanding would have occurred between our two countries.

Q: What are your thoughts on evacuation? What do people need to know?

Evacuation will probably happen to most people in the Foreign Service at some time. In the last three years there have been over 60 nations on evacuation status. Thousands of people have had their lives interrupted and put on hold. The most difficult part of evacuation is the loss of control and the uncertainty that people feel. I was evacuated from China, during the Tiananmen massacre.

Some important guidelines are to have a plan for where you plan to stay in the U.S. Maintain separate checking accounts and credit cards. Take an inventory of the belongings you have at post, and decide which items you would take with you in a suitcase in the event of sudden evacuation. You may want to leave invaluable items and mementos at home in the U.S. even before you go to post, just as a precaution. Maintain copies of all your important papers back in the U.S. as well as two copies at post (one for you and one for your spouse). Have these documents readily available.

Keep connected with people in the United States and keep them informed of your whereabouts. Make sure you get all the insurance you can, including: household effects insurance at post, in storage and enroute; health insurance for all family members; disability insurance for employed members of the family; life insurance for an unemployed spouse; and car insurance, including collision and liability specific to the country you will be living in. Read the pamphlet "Evacuation Plan: Don't Leave Home without It," published by the State Department, and discuss your family's contingency plans in the event of an evacuation.

Q: How has your life changed since that terrible day?

Perhaps the most significant change I feel is that my family is very important to me. I do not want to be far from them. I realize in today's uncertain world, that the family is the only solace. If your family is strong, it doesn't matter that much where you live. I want to provide my family with a strong sense of warmth and love. This strong base will hopefully prepare each of us to contribute to a better world in our unique ways.

Q: Do you have any advice regarding safety overseas for newcomers to the Foreign Service?

The world has changed in recent years. It is no longer safe to be an American anywhere. It is not possible to say that it is safer to stay in the U.S. than to go abroad. In any place you may be a target of people who hate our country. The most important advice I can offer is to keep in mind that by living and working abroad, you can hopefully change some of the negative stereotypes that exist about our nation and in so doing, make the world a safer place for future generations. It takes courage and a spirit of adventure, but it is a patriotic choice. It is important to be aware that in many ways, as a Foreign Service Officer or family member, you are on the front line of international relations. This can be dangerous, but all will be grateful to those who take the lead in diplomacy and move the world toward greater understanding in a peaceful and personal manner.

When the War Began

by Patricia Hughes

Sanaa, Yemen
Thursday, May 5, 1994, 11:35 a.m.

There's no doubt now that civil war has come to Yemen. What a tragedy. Art [the ambassador and my husband] and the others had so hoped that it could be avoided, but evidently there wasn't enough *will* on either side to seek real solutions.

I am not sure what time we turned out our lights last night with hopes of sleep—it was after 12:30. Art had already talked to several cabinet ministers when the Prime Minister called. "The inevitable has begun," he said. The earlier calls had reported troop movements in various areas and possible fighting.

Art told me that if it weren't calm by morning with signs of some positive negotiating that he would decide on a draw-down. This meant evacuation for the families and most officers.

We were awakened by another phone call. And again by scattered gunfire. A mosquito woke us at three a.m. and we had to turn on the light and get out the bug spray!

Then to sleep again…to be awakened less than two hours later by anti-artillery fire. At first I thought I heard gunshots again and I slowly peeked around the curtains. I was fascinated to see "sparks" arcing over the sky. They were tracers—anti-aircraft fire. At that moment we heard a plane, or planes. Art was up and shouting "Get away from the window," and I hit the floor.

There was a hell of a lot of artillery noise and it continued even after the planes were out of the vicinity. Then began the phone and radio contact with the Marines and with various Embassy people around the city. No reports of anyone injured and no property damage. Art told everyone to stay home and "keep your heads down."

At 6:15 we received a call from Aden. The man told us that at 6:05 planes had begun making bombing runs over Aden airport.

We had the "feeling" that one of the planes that came over Sanaa earlier had dropped a bomb—judging from the horrendous sounds we heard—but that hasn't been confirmed.

During a quick breakfast, our State Department visitors decided that they should leave the country as soon as possible—today—but still hoped for a meeting with President Saleh.

After the men left for the Embassy [next door], I got out the bacon that was intended for tomorrow's American Business Association breakfast. I fried a kilo and a half of bacon, heated blueberry muffins and made toast. Abdul Hameed made coffee and we carried it all to the Embassy. About 15 people had come in, plus the Marines. They were hungry.

I have put the turkeys in the oven—stuffed. I know it was stupid, but I thought those birds just *had* to have stuffing. Besides, I dried and measured the bread yesterday. We had invited sixteen people for dinner tonight.

Unfortunately we are low on vegetables and fruit—Hassan [the cook] was to have shopped for these things this morning. When he called, we told him to stay home.

Thursday, May 5, 1:45 p.m.

I have just heard some shooting that sounded fairly close. It's the first I've been aware of for several hours, although I have been in the kitchen with the noisy fan on. We've packed a lunch for Bob, Jerry, their pilot and crew. The airport has promised them a speedy take-off clearance. Art has gone with Bob to see President Saleh—as far as I know.

Now the question is: how long will it take to get planes in and out of Sanaa? With spouses, children, Peace Corps and officers, we'll need a lot of seats. Depending on the situation, some airlines may not fly in here on their regular schedules. Probably not. We heard on Wednesday that Lloyds of London had canceled the insurance on any Lufthansa aircraft flying into Yemen.

Thursday, May 5, 9:14 p.m.

We fed turkey to about twenty people tonight with cranberries, canned vegetables and bread. Nothing elegant, but it filled a lot of tummies. I had only a few potatoes and the Marines got to them first. We sent tuna sandwiches to the Embassy for lunch. I lost track of how many cans I opened.

My daughter Kathy called [from the States] and I could hardly hear her because the triple-A was so loud. I had to sit on the floor in the library because there are no curtains on those windows.

Friday, May 6, 8:52 p.m.

It's been a long day and it's not over yet. In the past hour there has been anti-aircraft noise. There had been none all day.

We got some much-needed sleep last night. No phone calls because the lines were out, but we were awakened twice by shelling of some sort. It was loud, but didn't last long.

I heated the rest of the muffins this morning and took them, along with the big coffeepot, to the Embassy. Many of the officers, including the DCM, had spent the night there. A female colleague came over to sleep in our guest bedroom. I couldn't talk any of the others into coming over here.

The ABA breakfast was canceled, of course. We sent word out that—IF safe—all Americans were asked to come to the garden of the residence so that Art could give them as much information as possible.

People began arriving a 9:40 a.m. We made coffee in the 55-cup percolator and ran out, but we also offered tea, juice and cookies. It was a good session with Art and other officers explaining evacuation procedures. They recommended that all Americans leave. The Embassy will draw down to only essential personnel. At that time we didn't have information as to exactly *when* or *how* this would be accomplished.

Now, however, we know that it will be tomorrow. I don't want to go.

It was noon before people left. I had to lock the doors—literally—because people wanted to mill around and chat. Comfort in numbers, I'm sure. I needed to get rid of everyone so we could get food ready to take to the Embassy for lunch.

Since our Fourth of July order of hamburgers and hot dogs (from the Riyadh commissary) had arrived last week, I thawed out several pounds of hot dogs and sliced our last loaves of bread—that was lunch. We had pickles, but no fresh veggies. Someone had unloaded the Economics Officer's freezer and refrigerator—no electricity in most of the city. She had lots of cheese so I took some to the troops, with crackers.

Sossi, the CLO, arrived later with the contents of their freezer. It was thawing so I made sandwiches with some of it—including the smoked salmon. Fortunately she brought vegetables, so scurvy and rickets have been avoided for another day. There's enough food in my freezers to feed the guys for months!

I realize that this writing is becoming food-oriented—but in a crisis everyone has a job to do, and mine is "feeding."

Hamburgers and buns are thawing, baked beans and zucchini are ready—but no one has shown up yet. Too busy to eat. Art just called to say they still have some food at the Embassy.

I need to make lists for Art—what to do about certain things—in case I don't come back to Sana'a and he has to pack out by himself. I have avoided thinking about leaving. [I thought I was "essential personnel."] This is the pits! And it is much more difficult for families with children than it is for us.

Friday, May 6, 10:12 p.m.

Looking out the window toward the west is like looking into a black hole. No light anywhere. Last night, there were a few dull glows—probably from buildings with generators. Tonight nothing. Looking east, an occasional car goes by in front of the Embassy. Traffic had diminished even before the shooting started. Petrol has come by tanker truck much less frequently than before. Hassan said he waited all day yesterday at the station and could only get five gallons. Cooking gas has also been scarce.

Hassan made seven loaves of bread, cooked some shrimp for the troops and then had to head home before the six p.m. curfew.

Sunday, May 7, 12:50 a.m.

I left the house fifteen hours ago, and it will be at least another fifteen before we arrive in Washington. We're waiting for takeoff on a Saudi airliner.

I found out late Friday night that I was leaving with everyone else, and we had to meet at the Sheraton at 10:00 a.m. on Saturday for "processing" before going to the airport. Our Embassy people did a fantastic job getting everything organized—a major task.

We waited an hour and a half in the buses and it was hot. As soon as word came that the planes were approaching, we left for the airport and got out on the tarmac. We took our suitcases—one each—from the trucks and quickly boarded the C-130s. We took off at 2:55 p.m. A fueling stop in Taif gave us a chance to use the bathrooms and have a cold drink. We had eaten MREs during the flight. Off to Riyadh where we landed at 8:30 p.m.

A warm welcome awaited us by members of the Embassy staff, including Chargé David Welch and his wife, Gretchen, the Consul General. They did an admirable job. At the airport there was a play section for the kids, a diaper changing area complete with diapers, tables and chairs set up and helpful people to assist with paperwork. And food, cold drinks—and comfort!

Morale has remained generally good (except for two incidents) even though everyone is exhausted. Several kids have had airsickness, others diarrhea and nearly all the little ones suffered pain in their ears with the change in air pressure on the C-130s. And saying goodbye to daddies and one mother in Sana'a was tearful and stressful.

Art came to the airport and told people goodbye, solved some minor problems, and carried my suitcase onto the plane. I had a few difficult minutes—it was hard to say goodbye—but he feels confident I will soon be back in Sana'a.

Sunday, Mother's Day, May 8, 7:35 p.m. Eastern Standard Time On an Amtrak train from D.C. to New York City

We arrived safely. Morale picked up as we approached New York and then D.C. We were happy to be home.

Problems had pursued us, however; after boarding the aircraft in Riyadh we waited over two hours before takeoff. The flight was fourteen hours. I think there were 180 evacuees aboard. I tried to find all our Embassy people—especially those with kids—and check on them several times. After the C-130s, this plane was comfy and most of us got some much-needed sleep. Four hours for me was a blessing.

We landed in Bangor, Maine to refuel. After waiting an hour for this procedure, the pilot announced that there was a mechanical problem and we had to deplane. They might have to send a mechanic from New York to repair the problem. At this point many of the mothers were about to "lose it." We had been in transit for over 32 hours and another delay was just too much.

I asked a few of our State Department people if anyone had the phone number for the Operations Center. No one did. I *should* have had it! Sossi found the airport manager who located a quiet room with a phone for us. After many false starts, I reached a duty officer at the OPS Center and told him where we were. I suggested that if this wait lasted several hours, they make alternate arrangements for some of the mothers. The panic in my voice suddenly gave way to suppressed giggles. I don't know why. Fatigue? Or relief—just to be doing something useful.

Our flight was announced just as we came out of the little office. Off we went to Dulles International Airport.

I fell asleep then and that was the end of my diary. I had decided that I didn't want to stay in Washington. It was Mother's Day and I longed to see my children. I traveled for another three and a half hours to be with my daughter in New York City. I was glad I did.

The Unthinkable Can Happen: Divorce in the Foreign Service

by Ruby E. Carlino

Marriages fall apart every day in the United States. In fact, according to recent reports, one in two marriages end in divorce. The good news is you have a 50 percent chance of growing old gracefully in sunny Florida or some small town in America with the person you married. If you fall into the other 50 percent, however, divorce can be devastating and disastrous, both emotionally and financially. And if you're in the Foreign Service as an accompanying spouse, chances are you've given up your career to follow your employee-spouse all over the world. Bringing up your children in Ulanbaator, performing volunteer work in Kampala, and being an outstanding host or hostess in Istanbul may make for an interesting life, but hardly a great resumé.

Louise (not her real name) is fifty years old, and not a day passes when she does not worry about her financial future. Her FSO husband divorced her after twenty years of marriage. When her husband joined the Foreign Service, she willingly gave up a budding career to accompany him. Louise became a financially dependent spouse, raised four children, and except for a year here and a year there when she had a temporary Embassy job, she was a homemaker, as well as a hostess for her husband's official dinners and receptions. Looking back on the divorce process, she admitted that the shock of finding out her husband was gay right after returning to the U.S. affected her usually sound judgment. When he asked her to sign a quitclaim to his pension in exchange for their house in Falls Church, she did. It turned out she could not afford the mortgage and had to move to a smaller house.

Although Louise had worked for the government overseas, she did not have the required time to qualify for Executive Order Eligibility. This, plus the hiring freeze at the State Department, had severely limited the jobs available to her. Today, Louise works as a contractor for the State Department. She admits the Department still feels like home to her.

Christine (not her real name) was married for 26 years. Her FSO husband filed for divorce in the early 1990's and fought hard to keep her from getting any part of his pension. In court, he alleged that she had not assisted him in his representational duties, that she had abandoned the marriage when she did not accompany him to his last post, and that she did not deserve any part of his pension. She had to ask friends to vouch for her life in the service. Her divorce was finalized after four years of contentious wrangling and $40,000 in fees from her own pocket. She eventually received part of his pension. But he successfully argued that the marriage was over long before the divorce was filed, and as a consequence, the pension was computed for fewer years than they were actually married.

Christine also never thought that the man she married would do something so underhanded. When her husband hustled her to quickly sign a piece of paper, she did. She realized later on that she had signed away her rights to survivor's benefits. Today, Christine is 65 years old and working as a music teacher. She is still putting her daughter through college. She has expressed relief that she had a profession to fall back on; that she had thought of her finances before divorce was an issue, but she admits that she cannot retire as yet.

When you are in a happy and strong marriage, you rarely think about divorce. You don't go out expecting to get run over by a car, either, but like millions of Americans, you consider it prudent to purchase accident insurance. Think of knowledge as a kind of insurance, and treat the following as a preparedness exercise that, hopefully, you will never need.

A SAFETY NET: Be Prepared

Have your own checking/savings account, or consider setting up a trust account. Assuming that you enter the FS in good financial shape, and unless you are consistently posted in high cost-of-living posts like Geneva or Vienna, it would be close to impossible not to have any savings while overseas. Even if you work part-time or are self-employed, make an effort to fund your own savings/checking account, separate from your employee-spouse. If you're a full-time homemaker, consider putting the family's emergency fund into your savings account or putting away a specific amount from your household budget as your savings.

Get a credit card in your own name. Instead of getting a credit card through your employee-spouse, apply for your own credit card. Use this card when you shop online or for other specific expenses, in order to build up your credit rating.

Build your own retirement account. In planning for your retirement, note that the average life expectancy of women in America is 79.5. This is 5.7 years longer than men. Women over 65 often live under the threat of poverty. The Supplemental Security Income (SSI) from Social Security is just that, supplemental, and cannot be expected to be your sole source of income.

It is a fact that women are typically paid lower wages than men. The situation is exacerbated when you are overseas because of limited employment opportunities. Unless you are part of a tandem couple, your employment while accompanying your employee-spouse overseas will be intermittent at most. Even in the best of circumstances, when you can find a job with the mission, you will probably never earn more than $25,000 annually. This translates to fewer retirement benefits. The result? The amount of your Social Security payments would be lower than your employee-spouse's, and lower than those of other women who have lived and worked in the U.S. Men who are accompanying FS spouses are faced with this same dilemma, a situation that would not be true if they were in the U.S.

So if you don't want to be poor or a burden to your family in your golden years, consider your financial future carefully. A full-time homemaker is now eligible for a Spousal Individual Retirement Account (IRA) contribution. And if you work in a job that doesn't have a retirement plan but your employee-spouse does, you are still eligible for a fully-deductible IRA. Check with a financial adviser or with your financial institution for details.

Join an investment group or start one. Or if you are working, even part-time, consider signing up for a direct investment program. What you don't get, you can't spend. Even if you build up your portfolio very slowly, it will still amount to something someday. If you are a full-time homemaker, get your employee-spouse to fund the investment in your name. You can contribute for as little as $25.00 per pay period in some cases.

Get to know post management personnel. Some spouses do not like hanging out at the Embassy. Even if you are pursuing other activities and interests outside the American mission, make an effort to get to know the people your employee-spouse works with. Pay special attention to the Personnel and Administrative Officers. In the event of a separation or divorce, you will need their assistance in various ways, not the least of which is returning you and your children to the U.S. at the government's expense.

Maintain your personal ties to your home country (for foreign-born spouses). After years of leaving parts of yourself in exotic and dangerous places overseas, you may eventually feel America is home. You may never return to your home country to live again. But do not sever or discard your ties there. One day, should you have to go back—whether out of desire or necessity—it would be best not to go home a stranger to your own country. The Internet makes communication a lot easier these days. Form an online group or join your home country-American association (e.g. Turkish-American Association).

Learn or update your marketable skills. You need to have at least one marketable skill. Take an online class on the Internet; pursue an advanced degree, or start/learn a business. Use every volunteer opportunity to advance yourself in your field. Note that you can sign up for various courses (including computer courses) at the National Foreign Affairs Training Center when you are heading overseas but not when you are returning to D.C. Non-State Department spouses (USAID, FCS, USDA and others) should consult their own agency for training availability. (See the resource section at the end of this article for distance learning.)

Keep a record of your life overseas. Keep an album or a scrapbook of your life in the F.S.: where you were posted, what you did, where you went, who you saw and entertained, what was on the menu, etc. File away those Front Office "must attend" invitation cards. Document your volunteer work and don't throw away those "thank you" notes from the Embassy or other organizations that were the recipients of your unpaid labor overseas. These items are good to keep for the memories, anyway, but would also serve as proof of your life in the F.S. should it come into question.

Make sure you have a Joint Property Statement. "The Foreign Service Family and Divorce," a publication from the Family Liaison Office (FLO) explains and provides a sample of this document. Unless you have this, a power of attorney or a court order, you will not be able to retrieve your household effects from storage, because they are stored under the employee-spouse's name. This is a good document to keep in any case, should some other personal catastrophe happens and you need immediate access to your things. (See resource section at end of article.)

Work for the U.S. Mission while overseas, if a position is available. It is not only difficult to find a job that fits your qualifications at a U.S. mission overseas. As an accompanying spouse, you most probably will be hired on a temporary or part-time basis or will be underemployed. Note, however, that the work you do at an overseas mission can help you gain employment with the Federal Government upon your return to the U.S. (Executive Order 12721 on Noncompetitive Eligibility). This becomes extremely important should divorce become an issue, as this will widen your employment options. (See resource section at end of article.)

STREET-WISE: Be Aware of Your Rights and Existing Resources

Get an overview on divorce. Read "The Foreign Service Family and Divorce," a publication of the Family Liaison Office (FLO). This document is available online and can be downloaded from their website. (See resource section.)

Read the relevant portions of the Foreign Affairs Manual (FAM). This is not a complete list of sections in the FAM concerning divorce, but the following is a good place to start: (To access the FAM online, see resource section at end of article.)

2 FAM 221.5—Waiver of Immunity
6 FAM 126.2—Special Travel for the Departure of Spouse and Children From Post Before the Employee
6 FAM 126.10—Return Travel of Spouse and or Dependent Children to the U.S. in Connection with Divorce or Marital Separation
3 FAM 3750—Travel of Children of Separated Families
3 FAM 4139.9 Standards for Appointment and Continued Employment—Financial Responsibility

Disciplinary action may result when an employee's failure to fulfill his/her financial obligations result in embarrassment or discredit to the State Department or the Government. This section can be used as reference when demanding child support and alimony payments.

(See resource section at end of article for child support enforcement handbook and how to access the FAM via the Internet.)

Go online. There are many websites dealing with the issue of divorce, providing guidelines, advice, support groups, lawyer referrals, state requirements and other information. In the absence of close family members and friends overseas, you may find it necessary to use online resources to obtain guidance, information or support. (See resource section at end of article.)

IF YOU FACE A PERSONAL CRISIS: You're On Your Own

Grab life with both hands and listen. If you feel your marital life is spiraling out of control, don't hide in the closet. Face up and listen to the conversations with your guts: hear what he's saying, what you're saying back, how he is saying it, how you're responding back. Rebecca Bilbao, moderator of the online expatriate spouse e-mail group Spousesview advises: "Don't go for counseling with the notion that the counselor can referee and make things better. Go so you can hear yourself think and hear what you need to know and get validation and support for taking the appropriate steps to start repairing the situation or getting free of it. Go online, use books and journaling, go during home leave, but find someone to talk to, someone who will let you hear the truth and face it with courage. Marriage takes two people, and if one person thinks it's over, it usually is. Hanging on, holding out, being perfect, staying in control, but ignoring what you really need to take care of yourself is counter-productive."

This is your life, no one else's. During the divorce process, recognize that you may get emotional and irrational. Remember to consider all your options, think things through and make an informed decision based on facts. Do not get swayed into letting others make important decisions for you.

Look out for yourself; no one else will. After years of being told where and when to go, where to live or which school to send your children to, you might be lulled into thinking that the State Department will take care of you when divorce becomes an issue. Don't. The State Department views divorce as a personal matter. You can avail yourself of services provided by the Employee Consultation Service and the Family Liaison Office (FLO). FLO provides information, makes referrals, offers resources and advocates to resolve issues equitably. Note, however, that there are limits to what these offices can do for you. For example, FLO cannot provide you with a lawyer nor can it recommend one. (See sidebar.)

Do not expect people to take your side. Do not burn your bridges or force friends to choose your side during a divorce. Talk if you must, but keep in mind that the contacts and relationships you have in the FS could be a lifeline when the time comes for you to consider your employment options later. Networking is key. You never know when a particular person might lead you to a much-needed job.

LAST WORDS: Things to Remember

On Leaving Post

Don't leave post on your own without proper authorization from post management, even if you know your marriage is about to fall apart. You could be accused of abandoning your employee-spouse or kidnapping your children, or end up spending substantial sums of money if you don't follow the correct procedures. Be sure to contact the Embassy's Administrative Officer and the FLO for guidance before you make any travel plans.

On Lawyers

Be aware that not all lawyers are well-versed on divorce in the Foreign Service context and many may not be knowledgeable about your rights. Learn as much as you can and be an informed and active participant. For example, certain FS spouses are eligible for retirement and health benefits under the Foreign Service Act of 1980; during the divorce process you also have the right to access your employee-spouse's employment record.

On Survivor's Benefits

When your employee-spouse retires, you are normally entitled to a widow's benefit if he or she dies before you—unless you sign away your rights to a survivor's benefit or if he or she opts for lifetime benefit or a single lump sum payment, both of which eliminates the widow's benefit. If your employee-spouse chooses the lifetime benefit or the single lump sum payment, a signed spousal consent form will be required from you. (See resource section at end of article.)

On Estate Tax

U.S. estate tax law eliminates the unlimited marital exemption for surviving spouses who are not U.S. citizens. If you are a green card holder or a third country national, you and your spouse should consult a qualified estate tax professional to avoid this hidden marriage tax.

The unthinkable can happen even in the quiet corners of marital paradise. The best and the brightest can do painful, underhanded things sometimes. As a "dependent," "trailing," or "accompanying" spouse, you owe it to yourself to be prepared for every eventuality, including being on your own, and having to start over.

The emotional and financial burdens on the family make any divorce a difficult process to handle anytime, anywhere. The sad and sometimes horrible stories certainly afflict not just families in the Foreign Service. And although there may not be too many happy-ending divorces (particularly when there are children involved), some divorces are settled on friendly or amicable terms. A male FSO and his foreign-born wife mutually agreed to a divorce after five children and several years of marital woes. They agreed on joint custody of the children with the father as the primary caregiver and the wife electing to remain overseas. They remained on speaking terms, and both have since remarried. Should the unthinkable happen, is there life after marital death? Christine (mentioned earlier in this article) has more music students than she can handle. She has published an ear-training program and holds music workshops. Louise (also mentioned earlier in this article) has recently passed both the written and the oral exams and is currently waiting for a spot in an upcoming A-100 class. Louise, resilient ex-Foreign Service spouse, will soon be Louise, Foreign Service Officer. Is there life after divorce? Sure there is—but it is a lot easier if you arrive packed and prepared.

WHAT FLO CAN DO FOR YOU

Offer information and confidential guidance on:

- Departure from post

- Statement of mutual consent before departing post

- Rights of spouses, including foreign-born spouses

- Accessing storage

- Health insurance

- List of lawyers in the Washington D.C. area

- Mediation

- Garnishment of wages

- Custody issues

WHAT FLO CANNOT DO FOR YOU

- Offer legal advice

- Recommend a lawyer

- Lend you money

- Take sides—but it can advocate for equity

FLO has advocated in individual situations on such issues as:

- Temporary separate lodging at post

- Service of papers at post

- Spouse's right to a portion of the couple's household effects (HHE)

- Abandoned spouses

- Child abduction

ONLINE DIVORCE RESOURCES

Associates of the American Foreign Service Worldwide (AAFSW), www.aafsw.org. Check the FS Toolkit for an electronic version of the Foreign Affairs Manual (FAM). AAFSW also has a group called *Women in Transition*, but this is not an actual support group. Volunteers who may be interested in reviving the group or forming an online support group should contact Nancy Longmyer: **nanlong@msn.com.**

Family Liaison Office (FLO), www.state.gov/m/dghr/flo/. The FLO has a Support Services Officer (SSO) who can offer information and referrals as necessary. Email **flo@state.gov** and request that your email be forwarded to the SSO. You can click on Resources, then Publications and scroll down to the section on Support Services to download "The Foreign Service Family and Divorce" (State Department Publication 9914). Click on Family Support Services, then Divorce to view other divorce-related information such as garnishment of wages and a separation fact sheet.

This is also the site to download FLO's information sheet on Executive Order 12721 on Noncompetitive Eligibility. Click on Resources, and then scroll down to Family Member Employment.

First Gov for Workers, www.workers.gov/. Provides one-stop information on retirement and social security benefits, including family member rights and benefits and laws on pension and welfare benefits. Also offers information on distance education.

Women and Pensions, www.pueblo.gsa.gov/cic_text/money/ women-pensions/women.htm. An online "What Women Need to Know and Do" from the U.S. Department of Labor, with a pension checklist and a list of publications that can be requested from the Pension and Welfare Benefits Administration's toll-free Publication Hotline: 1–800–998–7542.

Handbook of Child Support Enforcement, www.pueblo.gsa.gov/cic_text/children/childenf/index.htm An online handbook on enforcement of child support.

The Divorce Research Center, www.divorceresource.com Offers extensive materials on divorce including a search function for lawyers, a research center, divorce laws and articles, forms and handbooks, a State guidebook and a download center for other informative materials.

The Women's Center, www.thewomenscenter.org. Provides a comprehensive range of services to support women, men and families coping with the emotional, financial and legal aspects of separation and divorce. The Center also offers referrals for free telephone consultations with three divorce attorneys in the Washington D.C. area (20 min. with each attorney) and sponsors support groups.

Motley Fool, www.fool.com. Offers plain-English financial advise on personal finances, retirement, and investment strategies, including several online self-paced seminars on finances.

Nolo, www.nolo.com. A website tailored to deliver self-help legal information, Nolo offers legal guides and forms for easy download, a law center and encyclopedia with articles on various legal topics, including "Marriage and Living Together" and "Divorce and Child Custody," and books and software for devising your own legal documents.

Major credit reporting agencies. For a fee, the following allow you access to your credit report and FICO credit score (or your spouse's) and offer the following additional services: **Experian (www. experian.com/consumer/index.html)** has a Credit Education section including a Fraud Center. **Equifax (www.econsumer.equifax.com/ or www.equifax.com)** offers Equifax Credit Watch to protect you from identity theft. **TransUnion (www.transunion.com/Personal/ OrderCreditReport.asp)** provides various delivery options for credit reports, and also offers a Fraud Victim Information section.

Life in Limbo

by Jennifer Kolodner

A warm breeze blows through my hair, scented with the heady perfume of the tropics…The bouncing tones of steel drums beat out a carnival rhythm, keeping time with swaying hips and waving arms…

A single bead of condensation dribbles down my hurricane glass of punch and drops, noiselessly, into the powdery white sand, as two well-muscled youths approach the crowd carrying a six-foot pole…

A riotous voice calls out to the crowd…

EVERYBODY LIMBO!!!!!!!!!!!!!!!!!!!!!!!!!!!!!!

As the crowd responds enthusiastically, clapping and whooping and yelling, one man's voice can be heard over the din. He calls out, in a clear tone, "Honey, have you seen my good shoes?" Huh? I shake my head in confusion, only half-understanding his words.

He continues, without missing a beat, "Do I even have a tie? Is it in your suitcase? Looks like I'm going to Main State tomorrow in hiking boots and my polarfleece. Yeah, that'll look real good. I think I have to hang a sign around my neck that says, 'Please forgive my attire. I'm an evacuee.' Whaddaya think? Honey? Honey?"

The dreamy fog lifts, leaving nothing behind but the dawning realization that we are indeed in limbo.

We own a lovely house.
We can't live in it because we've rented it out.
We own everything we could ever possibly need.
It's all on the other side of the world.

225

We've become accustomed to the rhythms and sounds of a foreign city.
We haven't had any music in our home since we packed out almost six
months ago.
We took six months of Arabic training before we left for Yemen.
It's steadily dissolving into babble from disuse.
I was fortunate enough to line up a job in our new city.
It's not likely to be mine when (if???) we return.
We were planning to have our families visit when we got settled in.
"Settled in" is an impossible concept. "Planning" is laughable.

My husband joined the Foreign Service about a year and a half ago
after a long bureaucratic process (as only the government can provide)
and a great deal of speculation on our part as to what our future would
hold. When we bid on Sana'a, Yemen for our first post, we knew more
than most Americans about the country; my husband had wanted to
visit Yemen, the stuck-in-time Arabia Felix, for as long as I'd known
him. And since this was before the attack on the USS Cole in Aden,
most people responded to our news with "Where?" or "Do you mean
Oman?" or "Isn't that where Chandler goes on that episode of
'Friends'?" While we weren't sure what the quiet, un-newsworthy city
would be like, we figured we could count on adventure, new challenges, and the great unknown of life far outside of the Beltway.

We talked everything out and were confident that we were making
this huge life change together, as a couple. As an Instructional Designer
of educational computer programs, I was unsure if I'd be able to find
something in my field, but as everyone kept saying was required for a
Foreign Service Spouse, I was ready to be flexible. Maybe I'd become a
teacher or an educational consultant. Maybe I'd get more involved in
technology work. We made a deal: we'd give it a shot and if either of us
was miserable, we'd chalk it up to "well, we tried" and move along. But
whatever we did, we'd do it together. That was the important thing.

After the bombing of the USS Cole, we started to get nervous about
our destination but we soldiered on. That was Aden, we said; we're
going to be living in Sana'a. Two totally different places, we told our-

selves. Several months later, just as we were preparing to leave for Sana'a, the Embassy decided to go to Authorized Departure status: any non-essential personnel and family members were authorized to leave on the government's dime if they so chose, but anyone who wasn't yet in Yemen had to wait to travel there until the authorization had been lifted. This delayed us by about 6 weeks, but we signed up for another few weeks of language training and waited it out, enthusiastic but cautious now.

We arrived in Yemen eager to make it work. My husband dove into his work at the Embassy. I ventured out with another "wife" and got to know the neighborhood and then started my job at AMIDEAST, a U.S.-based nonprofit. After a few weeks, my husband and I returned to the States for the wedding of some dear friends, a short trip we'd planned months in advance. We arrived in New York on September 8. On September 11, the whole world changed. The Embassy returned to Authorized Departure status on September 19. We've now been here for three months and authorization has just been continued for another month. My husband has now been ordered to return to post without me. I have no idea what to do.

Emotions are running high, but in all different directions. Above all, we are grateful that we are together so far, when so many evacuees are separated from their spouses. Then again, we're frustrated and upset that my husband will soon return to Yemen without me. While we're glad to be home when leaders are talking of war, we yearn for more time in Yemen to develop new friendships, buy mementos, explore. We also miss our spacious Sana'a home, a veritable palace compared to what we could afford in the States. Then again, we're not sure if we'd be safe there (there wouldn't be an authorized departure unless there were some credible threat against Americans) and we have no desire to be heroes or targets. Should we curtail? Should we return? We just don't know what the right decision would look like. We're starting to understand why Yemenis end each forward-looking sentence with

"Insh'allah"—God willing. Humans have little control over their lives, and it is experiences like this that bring that message home.

To be honest, it's oddly embarrassing to be back so soon. Our impending departure for our first post was a shared experience for our community, a major source of excitement and trepidation that we all anticipated, and got used to, for over a year. During that time, we celebrated the present, imagined the future and completely exhausted our capacity to say goodbye, goodbye, goodbye, until we wanted everyone to just go away—or for us to finally go away. And now we're back. Our adventure has turned to frustration, a feeling one is not so inclined to share with an expectant crowd. We know we haven't done anything wrong, that we're just boats tossed upon the waves, and yet we feel like we've somehow disappointed them and ourselves by returning home so quickly.

Thankfully, our relatives don't see it that way and are glad to have us back so soon. Despite September's violent attacks here at home, they breathe a sigh of relief when they see us, as if their love, in direct proximity, can protect us from harm. "Nothing's blowing up at post," we joke back at them, with uneasy laughter. "(Yet)," we quietly acknowledge to each other only, thinking of our colleagues who are still working hard at the Embassy.

Our friends see every night out as either a "bon voyage" party or a "welcome back" celebration. But some become irritated at our inability to make firm plans and our "wait and see" attitudes. "If you've been here for three months already, how can you call that limbo?" one asks. She just doesn't understand that each month, the day when we'll be told if the authorized departure has been lifted looms like a cliff we can't help but run toward. Past the crumbling edge of that date, nothing is solid. Nothing can be planned, everything is changeable. Whether post reopens or we remain in evacuation status, it's all unknown past that point. Each 30 days is like a leap of faith—without the faith. When a decision comes each month, we breathe a sigh of relief at the knowing. Not the information itself, just the knowing.

And while my husband is off to the State Department each morning where there's plenty of work to be done, here I sit at "home"—now a very flexible concept—contemplating the life we've begun and trying to decide if it's been a big mistake. Before we left for Yemen, I'd somewhat come to terms with the career and paycheck I'd given up. But now we're back and I'm faced with the impossibility of finding important and fulfilling work when one's life is parceled out in 30-day chunks. In my initial determination to make the most of my time here, I found a job, but quickly realized the futility of that plan: no one's going to give interesting work to the new person who doesn't know how long she'll be around. I took pottery classes, I ran errands, anything to keep busy. But doing laundry should not be the high point of anyone's day. I've looked into volunteer work, but that requires a time commitment as well. I thank God that I never liked alcohol much because this situation could drive one to drink, and depression looms as a very real threat. With this as my introduction, is it any wonder that my enthusiasm for Foreign Service life in general is flagging?

From discussions with friends, colleagues, and the Livelines support network, I've determined that the instability that I'm attributing to evacuation status is a concentrated dose of the normal ups and downs of the Foreign Service lifestyle. Fortunately, most people don't walk straight into that realization on the first tour, or recruitment and retention would be even thornier problems than they already are. It's very hard to imagine how this will play out. Perhaps this experience will inoculate us, making all future posts seem easy in comparison. Or maybe it will sensitize us, making us more aware of the difficulties of life abroad in government service. Like everything else in our lives, that remains to be seen.

The Move from Hell: Depression in the Foreign Service

by Victoria Hess

Two days after arriving at post, I crumpled to the floor of my living room, screaming and crying to my husband that I couldn't do it. I just couldn't do it. He insisted that I calm down and get off the floor: that I pull myself together. After all, he said, the electrician, a man who would be helping take care of us for the next two years, was waiting outside our house. Waiting to come in and fix some of the many problems we had found with our house in our first hours there. And it wouldn't do for him to find me in *that state*.

I didn't care. Really. The problem wasn't the electricity, or the house, or the jet lag. The problem wasn't my son, although when he asked for a glass of milk at dinner, I ran to my bed, curled up in a fetal position, and cried. It wasn't the lack of a social group, though the expat community had deserted post for the summer. It wasn't the move to a hot, dirty, dusty, unwelcoming, uncomforting, high-risk, and high-differential post at the end of the world.

None of this mattered, and it all mattered terribly, as I fell into a deep depression within days of our arrival at our fourth overseas post.

The Dark Side of the Foreign Service

When you are first starting out in the Foreign Service, the last thing you want to think about are all the things that can go wrong. There are

231

plenty. You or a family member could need medical attention far from an adequate doctor. Your family could be evacuated from your homes, and leave everything behind, on very short notice. Divorce happens no less frequently (and perhaps more often) than in the non-expat community. And depression, that medical condition that few understand, can rear its ugly head.

It doesn't matter who you are or where you live. Depression is a fact of life for eight percent of American adults, 20 percent of women. There is nothing special about the Foreign Service lifestyle to shield you from this, but there is plenty that can make coping with it seem more difficult. Though I have spent plenty of time blaming my depression on where I am and how we live, the fact is it could have happened anywhere, any time. Though I believe that perhaps the stress of the move and the lifestyle made it more acute more quickly.

Dealing with Culture Shock

If you were lucky, before your first overseas post you received the standard orientation to culture shock: the first weeks at post are exhilarating. This is followed by a period of let-down and disenchantment. Then, after a number of months, one generally becomes comfortable with the differences of the foreign environment, and one settles down to life in the new city, until it is time to disengage two to three years later. This became a common experience for me in our overseas postings. I had also experienced reverse culture shock when returning to the U.S. But none of this prepared me for what happened to me during that transfer.

In retrospect, I should have seen it coming. For months, I had announced our posting to friends and they had asked me how I felt about it. I said I was okay. It was what my husband needed at this point in his career. Why would they ask such a question? I can only guess that my whole manner showed an unwillingness to move.

Then I delayed getting ready for the packout and ended up shipping things I could never use at post (ice skates in the tropics?) and storing things that I needed. I never did get my airfreight properly sorted, and I was shoving things at the packer as he was taping boxes shut.

The Normal Stress of Moving?

I knew something was wrong before we boarded the plane. I bought two bottles of St. John's Wort, having read that it could help with mild depression. I knew I wasn't eating properly (I lost 10 pounds in a couple weeks, not a diet I recommend), and that I was anxious. But I was convinced it was the normal stress of moving and that if I just kept going and got us to post—to our new home—everything would be fine. I could relax then, and everything would be fine.

But it wasn't. Within days, I changed from Superwoman, capable of moving a family halfway around the world without losing any luggage (just a Beanie Baby or two), into a person I did not know. A person who couldn't eat; who slept, yet never felt rested; who couldn't stop crying; who couldn't function well enough to take care of herself, much less the school-aged children who were her responsibility while her husband was off at work. Setting up a household, hiring help, learning how to get around: I had done it all before, but now, it might as well have been Mount Everest.

I Wasn't Me!

It was painful. It was scary. I knew something was very wrong, and when I got the courage to talk to my husband about it, he admitted that he also knew. *"This isn't me!"* I said. *"This isn't me!"*

We didn't know what to do about it, but I couldn't continue the way I was. I was afraid to contact the Regional Psychiatrist (RMO-P). I was certain that he would order me back to the States, and I knew that I could not handle another trip halfway around the world. Furthermore, I had no place to go. We had sold our house, our car—everything—in preparation for this tour. And I knew that my husband would be deeply hurt if this, his career-enhancing assignment, was ruined because I couldn't handle it. It was hard for him to understand that I couldn't control what was happening. It was equally hard for me to understand.

It was too much, though, and we agreed that even with the risk of curtailment, I had to make the call.

"I need help!"

"I need help!" were among my first, tearful, words to the RMO-P. One of the first questions he asked was whether I was suicidal. I hadn't even thought in those terms, but the fact that he needed to ask gave me pause. I denied suicidal tendencies. I have since read William Styron's book on his own depression, *Darkness Visible: A Memoir of Madness*, and shuddered to recognize myself in there: thinking while driving down the street if it might not be easier to just turn my wheel a bit.

I found help. The doctor was amazing, diagnosing me over the phone and arranging for me to get medication to improve my condition. He called me every day to see how I was, then, as the drugs took effect, every few days. We did not have to curtail, though some who are depressed have to. As bad as I felt, I wasn't bad enough to need to be hospitalized or otherwise removed from my new home.

Yet the struggle was not over. We spent nearly two years at that post, with me on anti-depressants and anxiety drugs for the whole time. We moved to a new post, for which I believe I only got a medical clearance because of the presence of a good American-trained psychiatrist there.

A Light in My Tunnel

This second move (my fifth overseas) was almost as depressing as the earlier one. I wasn't on the floor, but felt crippled when it came to making friends and really learning my way around our new city. Fortunately, I did get in touch with that American-trained psychiatrist.

Drug treatment by the regional psychiatrist, though perfectly adequate as far as it went, was not enough. After some soul-searching I realized I needed more, and I am so grateful to have been able to get it.

I wish I had been able to get some good talking therapy when I was first depressed, because learning to identify and deal with the patterns that lead to my depression has made a vast difference in my outlook to life.

My story ends with a thought. Depression is not unique to the Foreign Service. But members of the Foreign Service are not immune to it either. The regional psychiatrists provided by the State Department are kept busy. Being overseas can make it more difficult to get treatment for this very scary condition, but it must not be ignored if it pops into your life. Depression affects men, women, and children, and what is really scary is that if you have suffered from depression, you are far more likely to experience a second episode. It is very important to recognize that this uninvited guest could enter your life during your Foreign Service career, and if it does, you should treat it as you would any other medical condition and get help. No career is worth ignoring this one. It can be a killer.

A version of this article previously appeared in The SUN (Spouses' Underground Newsletter), now Tales From a Small Planet, **www.talesmag.com**

PART VII
Returning Home

Re-Entry: A Twelve-Step Program

by Shannon Jamison

Washington assignments are actually the Foreign Service's "one sure thing" for two reasons. The regulations require a U.S. assignment after a certain number of years overseas, and if you bid entirely on Washington assignments, you will get one. Whether or not you're ready for one depends a lot on how you approach "coming home."

1. Think ahead—way ahead.

Our first Washington assignment came after 11 years in the Foreign Service, but to be honest, plans for our re-entry began after the birth of our first child six years earlier.

She was born on home leave after we returned from a two-year posting to Romania; my husband was beginning Japanese language training at NFATC to be followed by five years in Japan (a second year of language training in Yokohama then a four-year assignment in Nagoya). After that, I knew that a Washington assignment would be on the horizon, given the number of years we would have been "out," and looking at my new infant, I also knew I didn't want to live in temporary apartments the next time we came back.

To that end, I guessed how much money we would need to make a 20% down payment on a "normal" single-family house in the suburbs, divided it by 60, and then promised myself that when we were overseas we would make a monthly payment to savings to meet that goal. There were more than a few major changes in our lives in the six years that followed, including the demise of my husband's employer (the U.S. Information Agency) and his subsequent assimilation into the Department of State, the birth of our second child, a government shutdown, and more. At one point, there was even the possibility that my husband's position would be eliminated, tossing us back into the bidding process and wrecking my whole timeline. However, I still stuck to the savings plan that I believed would result in a home of our own after reentry.

2. Research Washington, D.C. as you would any other new post.

After the birth of our second child, my re-entry plans began in earnest. I tried to accumulate as much information as I could about Washington-area housing and schools. I e-mailed friends from previous posts who were back in Washington or had already done their first Washington assignment. I checked out **www.realpostreports.com** for the review of Washington neighborhoods and logged onto **www. realtor.com** to check real estate listings. Since our oldest child would be six the summer we returned, I began to research schools too. Fortunately, most of the Washington-area public schools have a wealth of information on their websites; many post the test scores of all the schools, as well as staffing and enrollment statistics. I also bought a book called *The Independent School Guide for Washington D.C. and Surrounding Area* to explore the private school option.

The actual re-entry process began with bidding, and mastering the intricacies of the Department of State bidding process for the first time was not fun. Still, my husband believed that working at main State was the best way to make the transition to his new employer, and that a Washington assignment, however initially difficult, would be the best way to learn to understand his new work environment. From both a work and family perspective, it was time to go "home."

3. Ask for advice.

Once his assignment was made, I began soliciting advice in earnest from everyone. AAFSW's Livelines was invaluable at this point, as were several of the friends I made through that forum. One of the great benefits of Livelines, and the Foreign Service community in general, is the wealth of experience out there and its accessibility to those in need. It was on Livelines that I was warned to begin the process of applying to preschools immediately because if I waited until after we actually returned to the States, I would probably not be able to find a place in the preschool of my choice.

This was mind-boggling to me. How on earth could I apply to preschools I hadn't seen? How could I even begin to select one when I didn't know where we would be living? However, I knew that my youngest child needed a social life too; the highlight of our week had been our English-speaking playgroup. I went back to my research to decide both what I wanted in a preschool and in which area we were most likely to live. After I had my criteria, I picked several preschools that fit and asked my mother (an early childhood education specialist) to call as many as she could to ask for application forms. A friend from Livelines was also extremely helpful, sending a brochure and application forms for her own children's preschool. We finally applied to three, two in Vienna and one in Falls Church. We were, in fact, put on a waiting list at first (we got in before the start of school)—and I thought how right everyone on Livelines had been. I never would have even thought to apply until after we had arrived, and then it would have been much, much too late.

4. Keep your own priorities in mind.

I also received good advice that just didn't apply to our situation, such as "Don't buy a house now, because it's a seller's market. Rent this time around and wait for a buyer's market." While financially sound, this advice conflicted with a real emotional and psychological need on my part. We wanted a home of our own, for ourselves and our children, even if—as turned out to be the case—it cost more than it was worth. I was also told "Have your kids join AWAL and/or Globe Trotters [groups sponsored by the Foreign Service Youth Foundation, **www.fsyf.org**]; it really helps the transition back to know other Foreign Service children." Unfortunately my children were not yet old enough for either group, but we did still strive to introduce them to other Foreign Service families anyway. We agreed that we all needed to know that living overseas was a normal way of life for other people too. AAFSW also organizes a playgroup for very young children which we attended a few times.

The advice that was often most valuable to me were points I hadn't considered or points that ran counter to typical advice. In the first category was "Look at all the schools—K to 12—for your neighborhood because you never know how old your kids will be on your *next* Washington assignment." I had been focusing on elementary schools because that's where my children would go, but I also began to look at middle schools and high schools, evaluating the whole "pyramid." One friend, also an education specialist, had changed houses and neighborhoods for their second D.C. tour because of the schools. She regretted that they had not been able to "come home" to the same house and same neighborhood, having to start all over again for herself and for her kids. That really resonated with me—echoing my own desire to give our kids a "home" in the U.S.—so I began to narrow my list of acceptable neighborhoods, crossing off the ones with great elementary schools that fed into middle or high schools that were less impressive.

In the second category was "Don't buy more house than you can afford; be very conservative." I had heard from a lot of people that financially their Washington assignment was the most painful. And that fact causes many Foreign Service types to keep their tours in Washington few and far between. Paying for your housing and your utilities for the first time in many years can definitely be a shock. Our first winter back was a rather cold one that was accompanied by very high gas and heating oil prices, and it seemed to me that our heating bill actually doubled each month as winter went on. There was definitely a point that I thought if it doubled again we would have to borrow money to pay it—the household budget just couldn't accommodate that kind of fluctuation. I knew I didn't want to have to become a miser, so the advice to be conservative in buying a house also resonated with me, although it ran hard up against my desire to buy the perfect house. I wanted the fairy tale ending—to have all that research and advance planning and careful saving result in the house of our dreams in an idyllic neighborhood with perfect schools and an easy, uncomplicated re-entry. (HA!)

5. Constantly reevaluate your expectations.

The last two or three years we were overseas were a boom economy in Washington. The whole area was transforming itself from a government town to a high-tech center and housing prices skyrocketed accordingly. I could even tell from **www.realtor.com** that the house and neighborhood we could have afforded if we had bought before we left for Japan would now be out-of-reach financially upon our re-entry. I also began to realize that we would need a lot more than a house—big-ticket items like a car and furniture were looming too. Like a lot of Foreign Service families, our first Washington assignment was the first time we actually needed our own beds, tables, chairs and sofas. We had some beautiful Romanian rugs, lovely Japanese antique chests, and absolutely nothing on which to sit. My careful savings were going to have to go much further than I had imagined.

It also was starting to become clear that we were going to be on a very tight schedule with some significant complications. There was a summit meeting scheduled in Okinawa for the end of July and all hands were being pressed into service. One option would be to wait until my husband returned from the summit to do the packout and travel to the States together, but that would put us very late into the house-hunting season, and give us very, very little time to buy a house and get settled before school started. The other option didn't seem great either—our children and I would leave immediately after school ended in late June, get over jet lag at my parents' house in Missouri, then travel to D.C. where I would buy a house with a power-of-attorney instead of my husband. Caught between a rock and a hard place, we decided I would go it alone. And we cut a deal. I agreed to make no criticism of the packout, which I have always handled and which would now be entirely up to my husband. He agreed not to criticize the house which I would be forced to find on my own.

Once the dates for our re-entry began to solidify, we started to make arrangements for all the details. I read all the temporary housing reviews on **www.aafsw.org** and got additional recommendations from friends. My husband made reservations for us at the Oakwood apartment complex in Falls Church, which was highly touted for being kid-friendly as well as close to the neighborhoods we were considering. The Oakwood was also very near my church, which I had joined when we entered the Foreign Service many years ago, and to which I was looking forward to returning. In addition, I made arrangements to spend the first week in D.C. house-sitting for my parents' friends to cover the entire time between our arrival and my husband's first day at his new job. We desperately hoped it would be enough time to complete our house purchase and move into our new home.

We also began to investigate the mortgage process, and discovered that several lenders were instituting referral programs so that we could also find a real estate agent even though we were 5000 miles away. Furthermore, the real estate agent was able to give us the specific power-of-attorney that was necessary for me to conduct a real estate transaction in my husband's name. She was very firm that a general power-of-attorney would not be sufficient, and we were able to have the specific one executed for me to hand-carry back to the U.S. Although my husband actually arrived before our closing date, I was glad that by finding a real estate agent in advance, and communicating with her in real time about our situation, we were able to avoid any complications and problems. (And it certainly would have been a problem trying to track him down at the summit conference to execute a correct power-of-attorney and send it to me before I could make an offer on a house.)

6. Preserve your memories.

Livelines was also the source of some excellent advice I received about preparing my children for our departure from Japan, the only "home" they had ever really known. I took lots and lots of pictures in our last few months, and we tried to do many of their favorite activities and visit their favorite places. I never said it was "for the last time," but I didn't want them to have regrets. We talked as much as we could about how it would be sad to leave, and how we would miss our friends, but also about making new friends and enjoying our new home. In some ways, it also helped that they didn't have to experience the packout. I was pretty unsuccessful in obtaining their consent to give any of their toys away; even ones that were complete outcasts became "favorites" when I suggested giving them to younger friends. It was much simpler to leave my husband notes about the most significant things that were not to be moved and then leave it up to him.

The day after the end of kindergarten, the children and I boarded a plane and our re-entry began.

7. Ask for help.

Traveling alone with two small children cannot be recommended. I asked for assistance from the airline and didn't get it. Fortunately, there was only one point where it was borderline disastrous—offloading the luggage and the children from an airport transit bus simultaneously wasn't possible, so I took the luggage off (better to leave that unsupervised at the curb than them I thought) but then I had to fight my way back on the bus to get my kids!! Fortunately, my parents met us on the other end, and we recuperated for several days at their house. This was especially good because my youngest spent the next few days vomiting profusely—a reaction to the stress of travel and jet lag. I was so grateful to my parents for their help from that point on—it made a world of difference to my children to have familiar beloved people to anchor their world while I dealt with all the tasks ahead.

After our days and nights synchronized with the world around us, we flew to Washington and moved into our friends' home for a week. My parents drove out the next day to watch the children and I began the house-hunting project. There were only about seven houses in our desired community available to us at that time, only one of which was in an elementary school district I preferred. That's the house I looked at first, and the house we eventually bought, so perhaps it was "meant to be." My initial reaction, however, was utter dismay because it was so small. It was definitely disappointing that all my careful planning and savings would not get us anywhere near my "dream house." I thought we might be the only expatriates to actually have had more living space in Japan than in our new house in America! I admit to great relief that I had completed my mission, even though I found it very hard to be enthusiastic about the house. Before we had even moved into our temporary apartment, I had found a home.

8. Be prepared for setbacks.

I remember our time at the Oakwood in a very hazy way—almost like the first few months after the birth of a child. There was so much to do—all the utilities had to be changed to our name; I needed to notify so many people and companies of our new address; I had to get my oldest daughter registered for school and finalize arrangements for preschool for my youngest daughter. And everything I tried to accomplish seemed to uncover another series of things I had to do. For example, both school registrations required physicals which necessitated locating a pediatrician. (Again I relied on recommendations I had received from Livelines—an invaluable help to me.) Summertime check-up appointments are hard to come by, and even after I submitted the forms, the school had a problem with my oldest child's immunizations—one shot had been given seven days too early. (I distinctly remember trying to get that particular series of vaccinations done before we left for Japan; who knew in the long term it would be unacceptable to Fairfax County?) So I had to go back and forth between the pediatrician and the school to resolve that.

The children were definitely experiencing a great deal of stress. I tried to be sure to give them as much attention as possible and to do things that were focused on them. We went to the Oakwood's "playgroup" as often as possible, and to the pool almost every afternoon. We watched Pokemon—their favorite TV show/phenomenon from Japan—almost religiously, and they both had Pokemon birthday parties. (We compensated for a lack of peers to invite by having both sets of grandparents and other extended family come.) Pokemon actually served as a bridge that summer—something from Japan that my children liked and knew a great deal about that was also familiar to every child that they met in the United States (although I found it misunderstood by most American parents.) I also tried my best to keep our children informed about the whole re-entry process; my mother brought them to see the house when we were having the home inspection and we took them to see both their schools. It helped them to have a mental picture of the things about which I was constantly talking.

Nevertheless, the extended time away from their father and the constant upheaval took a toll. My youngest child, who had been able to put herself to sleep since infancy, suddenly required someone's presence in the room to go to sleep—and still does. I will also never forget my oldest child, who is by nature calm and obedient, pitching a screaming fit about something insignificant. When I told her to "get a hold of herself," she looked at me in tears and said, "I can't," and we were both very disturbed to realize it was true. She had been pushed beyond her limits. We resolved that particular moment with a relaxing bath and extra story time, but I was made deeply aware how much I was asking of my children in this process, and I reminded myself again to focus more on their experience.

Needless to say, it was a great relief to be reunited as a family. When my husband finally arrived, we acquainted him with the Oakwood, laughing about its character as a Foreign Service ghetto. Virtually everyone we'd met so far was from the Foreign Service—some just starting training, some on pregnancy medevac (several actually!), some between assignments like us. We also tried to exchange all the details of our separate lives—he had lots to say about the packout and wrapping up our affairs in Japan; I had so much to tell him about the house and schools.

9. Plan to have fun.

We also realized that this brief time in the Oakwood was really all the family vacation time we would have that year. The closing on our house was scheduled for August 15th; my husband was to report for work on the 16th. If we wanted to do any sightseeing, or plan a special outing, we had to stop focusing on all the things we "needed to do" and seize the limited time we had. We decided that we needed a very kid-friendly outing—something to really get the children excited about our new location. The National Zoo seemed to be the perfect idea. We were very fortunate to pick a beautiful sunny day, and we began not far from the elephant enclosure. As we approached the elephants, one of the Zoo's peripatetic docents appeared and began to tell us all sorts of wonderful facts about the elephants—how old they were, what their names were, which were their favorite activities…She even had part of a tusk that had been trimmed from the African elephant and our children were delighted that they could touch it. We were also excited to hear that one of the elephants was pregnant. As we finally walked on to the next exhibit, after absorbing a fascinating lesson, I remember remarking to my husband, "And that was all in English!" After years and years of being limited and frustrated by my lack of language skills, I was thrilled to realize I was going to be able to understand everything here! I suddenly experienced a feeling of real excitement about our re-entry; until that moment, I had been so completely overwhelmed by everything that I felt I had to accomplish that I had not really enjoyed "coming home." The National Zoo will forever have a special place in my heart for that epiphany, and in recognition of that fact, my husband gave me a membership in the Friends of the National Zoo for my birthday that year.

The children were also able to attend Vacation Bible School each morning at my church during our last week at the Oakwood, an oasis of fun in a very hectic time. The closing on the house was the last leave day for my husband; we went immediately from the closing to the DMV to get new driver's licenses and then frantically began moving things from the temporary apartment to the house. Fortunately my husband's parents had come from Pittsburgh to help us. In three days' time we moved out of the Oakwood, received our small storage shipment, and accepted delivery of our air freight. To move up our closing date, we had agreed to acquire the previous owners' furnishings as well; they were finally retiring to their already completely furnished house in Florida. In many respects it was fortunate, because we had very little furniture to our own name—it was certainly nice to get a lawnmower and a grill—but it also gave us the rather creepy feeling of moving into someone else's house. We had to do a lot of "cleaning out" before we could do the "moving in"—twice the work I had anticipated.

The first two weeks in our new house was truly our time in "limbo"; the Oakwood had been temporary and had felt that way. This was supposed to be more permanent, but felt very isolated and unlike our life before in any way. We really missed the Oakwood pool and the loss of the television too. We didn't even have a phone at first, and although it was one of our first purchases, it took us some additional time to sort out which jacks went with which of our two lines.

It helped the children that we discovered a playground in a park at the end of our street—an unanticipated bonus of our location. We visited both schools, finishing the paperwork, and attended an Open House at each to meet their teachers. I had also made a point of enrolling them both in activities that would start with the new school year, so I could constantly remind them about the ballet lessons and soccer practice they would soon have. In the long run, I found it difficult to get the unpacking done because I felt I was always taking someone to this class or that practice, but I truly believed it eased the children's transition into their new home tremendously. In fact, I really had to resist the urge to sign them up for everything—ice skating, music lessons, art classes, swimming—all in English! Everything looked so appealing.

10. Acknowledge and accept mixed feelings.

I worried a lot about how the children would adjust to school. My oldest child was considered shy, a quiet introvert by nature. I was afraid she would be overwhelmed by the big elementary school, and I racked my brain to plan ways to help her make friends. I needn't have worried. She cheerily waved good-bye at the front door the first morning, and reported that she had three new best friends when she came home that afternoon. I was amazed—and infinitely relieved and happy. However, that first week of school was especially difficult for my youngest. She was considered the friendly, social one, an outgoing extrovert. I felt sure she would be fine once her preschool started, but the week before she began, she felt abandoned by her sister. They had always been friends and companions, but even more so this summer when they only had each other around. It was very difficult for her to see the older one branching out, and we all felt her pain. Even when preschool finally started, she still was unhappy that she only went three days a week, and she was unhappy to be home the other days. She said goodbye each morning at school without a fuss but her behavior at home was erratic, and it often seemed she was backsliding. She didn't want to sleep in her own room—she had been sharing a room with her sister at the Oakwood—and many nights she cried herself to sleep as we sat with her. "I want to go home!" she would sob, meaning to return to Japan, and it was so hard to have to explain that this was our new home. It was very painful for us to experience her grief, but we tried to acknowledge to her and to ourselves that her feelings were valid and she deserved to be heard. We always joke that her "volume" is just set higher than ours, but truthfully she felt the loss more deeply and expressed her loss more dramatically because of her nature. And even though her outbursts made me feel guilty and sad, I felt it would be a mistake to try to force her to keep a stiff upper lip or to be falsely cheerful. We just tried to be patient.

11. Hang in there.

The first year had some significant challenges. The State Department personnel office could not get its computer system to acknowledge my husband's new assignment, so we did not receive Washington-area locality pay. And even though the computer still believed he was in Japan, he did not receive the cost-of-living adjustment for our previous post either. Every two weeks he would take his earnings and leave statement to personnel to complain, and every two weeks he would be told that they would surely get it right next time. Six months later it was finally corrected, but not before there was significant damage to our savings. It didn't help matters that our furnace died in December and had to be replaced. I had heard so often that Washington was the most difficult assignment financially, and I had tried so hard to prepare for that fact. It was a double blow to experience a financial crunch in spite of all my efforts to avoid one.

There were some particularly difficult moments. I personally am averse to external chaos, and the clutter of half-unpacked boxes would periodically overwhelm me. One day I worked especially long and hard to get two boxes completely unpacked and put away. "Finally," I thought, "I have accomplished something. I have made some progress, albeit small, in clearing out this terrible mountain of stuff." I was thrilled because our youngest child had not bothered me at all while I was working, and so I had really managed to get something done. When I found her, she had taken her older sister's art class supply kit—in itself a precious reminder of a special part of our previous life—and she had covered the downstairs bathroom in oil paint and pastel crayons. I wept. It took me twice as long to clean the bathroom as it had to unpack those boxes—six steps backwards for every one step forward. And some of the damage was irreparable; the bathroom wall-paper had to be removed completely. Another day she drew on her bedroom wall with crayon, and it was many, many months before I could find the matching paint and repaint the wall.

After each of those times, I would just despair that things would ever get unpacked. Each Friday a few more cardboard boxes would make it into the recycling, but more seemed to grow in their place. And worst of all, even when things came out of the boxes they often sat in a pile where the box had been. Our tiny little house didn't seem to have room for all the stuff we owned. We actually had shipped 7,199 lbs according to the manifest—out of an allowance of 7200 lbs. And the house was already rather full with the previous occupants' belong-ings. We had a garage sale to get rid of as many of their things as possi-ble, and took even more to a consignment shop and to charity. I finally gave myself a deadline of one year—anything not unpacked by then would be pitched, and slowly we worked to meet that goal. We still struggle with finding homes for things, and that still bothers me a great deal. (I console myself with the idea that I will get rid of it all the next time we move!)

12. Make new friends but keep the old ones too.

Our new location proved very fortunate in a number of respects, but most especially because of our neighbors. A new friend from Livelines and old friends from my husband's junior officer training class lived very close to our new house, and both proved to be welcoming angels, alerting us to all sorts of wonderful community resources and events. Through them, my husband joined a carpool, cutting both his com-muting time and cost to nearly nothing. (He doesn't even have to drive!) These Foreign Service friends answered my strangest questions

("Do you put lightbulbs in the regular trash here?") and patiently listened to me gripe about silly aggravations ("Why do they put annoying stickers on every piece of fresh fruit in the stores?") Those Foreign Service spouses also understood my unexpected joy in an independent existence—the small but real pleasure of getting your own mail in your own mailbox, or introducing yourself as you wish without reference to your spouse's employer or position. And the parents I met in the Vienna community, through school or our children's activities, were also warm and friendly; they were eager to recommend places to get haircuts or find obscure school supplies.

Vienna also proved to be a bonus, because we encountered so many Foreign Service families that we didn't feel odd discussing our experiences overseas. Yet it also proved to be a small-town kind of community and we met many of the same people over and over again at soccer or Brownies or the dance studio or my husband's church. We felt we "belonged" right away in that sense and it helped.

We are now well into our second year, and our experience here has in fact proved to be so positive that my husband bid on all Washington jobs again so that we will have another tour when this one ends. I admit that I had no desire to move again so soon, but this assignment is also such a good place for our children that we wanted to make it last for a while if we could. We know we'll be heading out again eventually, but for now, we're happy to be home.

Contributor Biographies

Jan Fischer Bachman has a B.A. in Spanish and Music from Wake Forest University and a post-graduate diploma in Music Therapy from the U.K. She worked as a music therapist in England for several years, then moved to Mexico City to work with a Mexican Christian community center in a very poor area of the city. While in Mexico, she re-met FSO Brian Bachman, a fellow WFU graduate, and they married in 1993. Subsequent FS assignments included Santo Domingo, DR (1993–1995); Washington, D.C. (1995–2001, during which time Jan acquired two girls and an MBA); Nassau, Bahamas (2001-present). In spite of numerous obstacles, Jan has worked at least part-time at every post, playing the violin professionally; doing writing, editing and translating work; starting her own desktop publishing and consulting company; and/or continuing with music therapy work. She dislikes the fact that our society values people according to their paid work. Her unpaid priorities include raising two girls, staying in touch with friends and relatives, trying to help other FS people, and working on how to live out her Christian beliefs.

Mette Beecroft and her family have been in the Foreign Service for 33 years and have served in a variety of posts, including SHAPE (outside of Brussels), Paris, Washington, Bonn, Cairo, Washington, Brussels (NATO), Ouagadougou, Amman and two unaccompanied tours for her husband in Sarajevo. She served as the first Deputy Director of the Family Liaison Office, established it in the Department and started to set up the Community Liaison Offices (CLO) on a worldwide basis. She has worked in a variety of other positions in the Department and overseas. Mrs. Beecroft has served on the AAFSW Board in a variety of capacities. She has just finished serving a three-year term as AAFSW President but will continue her involvement as President Emerita and as BOOKFAIR Chair. Mrs. Beecroft attended Wellesley, Middlebury and the University of Pennsylvania from which she received the Ph.D. She has received several awards recognizing work done to safeguard and improve FS quality of life which include the Department of State Superior Honor Award, a special commendation from the Department of the Army and the Lesley Dorman Award for sustained outstanding volunteer contributions to the AAFSW.

Margaret Bender is an Australian-born writer, editor and ESL teacher. Having accompanied her husband on postings to India, Germany, Israel, Sri Lanka, Austria, and South Korea, she now lives in Virginia. She has just published the book *Foreign at Home and Away*, a collection of in-depth, intimate profiles of foreign-born wives in the U.S. Foreign Service.

Sheri Mestan Bochantin has been in and out of the Foreign Service lifestyle over the past twenty years (Liberia, 1981–83; D.C., 83–90; Ghana, 90–92; D.C., 92–99; Czech Republic, 99–2002; D.C., 2002-?). Along the way, she built a business as a troubleshooting contractor in human resources, served four years as a Community Liaison Office Coordinator, and worked seven years as a trainer for the (then) Overseas Briefing Center (OBC) in the State Department's Foreign Service Institute. It was during those years that she amassed statistics, research, and personal experience with long-distance relationships and developed an OBC workshop to address that particular facet of Foreign Service life. She kept busy in Prague co-founding an American women's group and establishing an Embassy preschool, among other activities. Sheri is now a trainer, writer, and editor living in Northern Virginia with her husband and two young daughters.

Ann Morel Bushnell of Scotch Plains, N.J., accompanied her husband, John A. Bushnell, overseas in 1962 to Bogota, and subsequently to assignments in the Dominican Republic, Costa Rica, Geneva, Argentina and Panama before retirement in 1992. Ann enjoyed her active role as a Foreign Service Spouse abroad, serving in several different official roles on the Board of AAFSW while in D.C., and receiving the Ambassador's Award for outstanding volunteerism in 1987 in Buenos Aires. At present Ann is studying philosophy toward a degree at Marymount University, teaching Adult ESL for Fairfax County, and is tutoring ESL for The English Speaking Union while enjoying her eight grandchildren.

Ruby E. Carlino is a freelance writer who was born and raised in the Philippines. Her writing credits include publication in *American Diplomacy, Turkish Daily News, European Stars and Stripes, Tales From a Small Planet, Foreign Service Journal, The Washington Post* and several Philippine magazines and journals. She writes a monthly column, "Traveler Without Luggage," for a Philippine magazine. She is also an independent web designer specializing in personal web projects and CD-ROM publishing. She has accompanied her husband to FS assignments in Ankara, Istanbul and Washington, D.C., and together with a toddler and two cats, will trail after him once more to El Salvador in 2003.

Karen DeThomas' first overseas posting was to Tehran in 1978, which she calls "a rather tumultuous beginning." She reports: "I think the Department sent us to Bonn in 1979 as a thank you." This was followed by her favorite overseas posting: Mexico from 1985 to 1987. This was followed by three years in Ethiopia, and finally Austria in 1997. Until it became too dangerous for students to travel to school, Karen worked as a guidance counselor in an international school in Tehran. Since she spoke some Farsi, she also spent a few months in the Student Visa Section until President Carter ordered an evacuation of spouses in early February 1979. While in Germany, she began a graduate program in business administration at Boston University's Overseas Campus, receiving an M.S. in business in 1982. She worked as Community Liaison Office Coordinator in both Mexico and Ethiopia. Karen is the mother of two wonderful children.

Shawn Dorman is the AFSA News editor of the *Foreign Service Journal*, where her spouse employment article originally appeared in May, 2002. She was a Foreign Service Officer from 1993 to 2000. Her accompanying husband, Shawn McKenzie, worked in the public health field during postings to Bishkek, Jakarta and Washington.

Fritz Galt is a writer and editor who has lived abroad as a Foreign Service spouse for many years. His postings include Belgrade (1989–1992), Taipei (1993–1997), Bombay 1997–2000), and Beijing (2000-present). He is a founder of Tales from a Small Planet (**www.talesmag.com**), and his novels are available at **www.spythrillers.com** and **www.amazon.com**.

John Hampson has served as a Special Agent with the U.S. Department of State since 1986. His assignments have included the positions of regional desk officer in Diplomatic Security's Office of Counterintelligence Programs (Eastern Europe), Assistant Regional Security Officer at the U.S. Embassy in Moscow (92–94) and Regional Security Officer at the U.S. Embassy in Dublin (94–97). In 1997 he returned to Washington and earned a Master's Degree in Strategic Intelligence from the Joint Military Intelligence College. From 1998 to 2002 he served in the Washington Field Office as a unit supervisor. In this position, he supervised 19 special agents and focused on passport and visa fraud investigations. One of his greatest and rewarding accomplishments during this time was the development of a small unit to assist in locating missing children whose parents had illegally kidnapped their children utilizing fraudulent U.S. passports. In 2001, SSA Hampson was transferred to the DS Training Center, where he is Unit Chief for the Criminal Investigations Training Unit which instructs new Special Agents. He and his unit also provide logistic and instructor support to the three International Law Enforcement Academies in Bangkok,

Gaborone, and Budapest. SSA Hampson was recently elected President of the Diplomatic Security Service Agents Association (DSSAA). He is happily married to Gabrielle A. Hampson and has three small children.

Victoria H. Hess is a mother, lawyer, writer, editor, and website designer (in no particular order). She has been traveling the world on the Foreign Service ticket since 1988 and has lived in Iraq, Germany, India, the U.S., Pakistan, and Zimbabwe, traveled to dozens of other countries, and been involved in no less than four evacuations. Over the years she has been an active volunteer in her Embassy and Consulate communities, including serving on school and commissary boards, producing community newsletters both as a volunteer and on a contractual basis, and assisted in the numerous small ways that make a difference to life in an overseas community. She has also held positions as a Community Liaison Office Coordinator, commissary manager, and diplomatic pouch clerk. She is presently the Chief of Operations and Webmaster of Tales from a Small Planet and Real Post Reports, a pseudo-volunteer position. She has two sons and is stationed in Zimbabwe as of 2002.

Patricia Hughes grew up in Nebraska and graduated from the University of Nebraska. She has been married to Arthur H. Hughes for 32 years, serving as a Foreign Service spouse and "accidental diplomat" (the couple's daughter, Katherine L. Hughes, Ph.D., is author of the book *The Accidental Diplomat*). Patricia and her husband have been posted to Frankfurt, Germany (1965–67); Maracaibo, Venezuela (68–70); Bonn, Germany (73–76); Copenhagen, Denmark (80–83); The Hague, The Netherlands (83–86); Tel Aviv, Israel (86–89); and Sana'a, Yemen (91–94). After leaving the Foreign Service, the couple moved to Rome, Italy, where Ambassador Hughes has been the Director of the Multinational Force and Observers since 1998.

Joanne Grady Huskey is a cross-cultural trainer who founded her own company, Global Adjustments, in Madras, India. She has done training for the Overseas Briefing Center at the Foreign Service Institute, the Peace Corps, the Organization of American States and Save the Children Federation. Prior to her international work, in the United States she was the international director for Very Special Arts International, based at the John F. Kennedy Center. Her background includes work as a television producer for WGBH TV (PBS) and a stage actor. She has a Master's Degree in Human Development from Harvard University. She is the wife of Foreign Service Officer James Huskey, and with him has been posted to China, India, and Kenya. They have two children and are presently living in the United States.

Shannon Jamison "married the Foreign Service" in August 1989. She has accompanied her FSO husband on assignments to Belgrade, Yugoslavia; Bucharest, Romania; Yokohama and Nagoya, Japan, and back to the Washington, D.C. area. They have two daughters.

Douglas Kerr was born and grew up in London. He earned a B.A. in Economics and Politics from a British university, where he also met his wife, and an M.A. in Political Science in Canada. He has lived in Nova Scotia, Alberta, Connecticut and Ohio, as well as in Tallinn, Estonia, where he and his wife wrote a series of newspaper articles, called "Tallinn Tales," on expat life there. His wife joined the State Department in July 2000, and they are now halfway through their first tour in Warsaw, Poland. Douglas has a home-based custom woodworking business. Please see **www.starpointwoodworking.com** for more details. He has never taken a called third strike.

Francesca Huemer Kelly, a trained singer and freelance writer, is the Editor in Chief of Tales from a Small Planet, a non-profit web magazine and resource center for people moving and living overseas (**www.talesmag.com**). Married to FSO Ian Kelly since 1982, she is the mother of four children. The Kelly family has lived in Milan, St. Petersburg, Moscow, Belgrade, Vienna, Washington, Ankara and Rome.

Jennifer Baltaxe Kolodner holds an Ed.M. in Technology in Education from Harvard and currently works as Instructional Systems Specialist for the Transportation Security Administration. When her husband, Michael, joined the Foreign Service, the couple viewed it as an opportunity for shared adventure, and Jennifer quickly obtained an interesting job at their first post, Yemen. However, the evacuation and months of separation that soon followed caused them to reevaluate their plans, and Michael has since resigned.

Kelly Bembry Midura is a freelance writer, website designer, stay-at-home parent and Foreign Service spouse. She has accompanied her husband, Chris, a Public Affairs officer, to Bolivia, Guatemala, Zambia, El Salvador, Washington D.C., and the Czech Republic. Kelly maintains an archive of her published articles on expatriate life at her business website, Kelly's Web Studio (**www.kellyswebstudio.com**) and invites interested readers to pay her a virtual visit!

Debbi Miller has been a Foreign Service spouse since 1976, and has accompanied her husband to Milan; New York City (USUN); Paris; Bridgetown, Barbados; Wellington; New Zealand; and several tours in Washington D.C. She is also a professional singer and the mother of three brilliant, talented children. She loves yoga, gardening, animals, bridge, and (luckily) foreign languages. She would like to point out that her Foreign Service realities have not all been highlights: for instance, her family once lost an entire air freight shipment including a beloved antique clock, and she and her children have been held at gunpoint by an escaped murderer, among other unpleasant events.

Nam Nguyen has been a JAGS ("Just a Gay Spouse") since 1992, when he met his FSO partner through introduction by a graduate school classmate. He and his partner together have weathered postings abroad to Thailand and Vietnam, and domestically to Washington, D.C., Princeton University and, now, New York. Nam received his Masters at the Kennedy School of Government at Harvard University and has worked as a financial analyst, an investment banker, an art promoter and an independent art curator as he has relocated from city to city to be with his partner. He is currently biting his nails in anticipation of their next posting.

Pat Olsen, her husband Norman, economic officer, and their three children have spent most of their Foreign Service career overseas, serving in Kingston, Jamaica (1983–85); Oslo, Norway (85–87); Washington, D.C. (87–89); Majuro, The Marshall Islands (89–91); Tel Aviv, Israel (91–95); Geneva, Switzerland (95–99); Washington, D.C. (99–2000); and Chisinau, Moldova (2000–02). Pat has published articles on the Foreign Service lifestyle, taught elementary school, chaired a school board, run a recreation center, home-schooled, served as president of five international women's clubs, worked as mental health coordinator, tutored, and edited. She made her symphonic debut with the Moldovan Philharmonic Orchestra. She has independently studied Norwegian, Hebrew, French, and Romanian. In 1994, she won The American Association of Foreign Service Women's Secretary of State's Pin for Outstanding Volunteerism, Near East Asia. She is completing her Master's in Elementary Education through the Fast Train Program at George Mason University.

Jan Zatzman Orlansky is currently a research analyst at Westat in Rockville, Maryland. In Indonesia, she developed the English training program for the Foreign Service Nationals (FSNs) at the U.S. Agency for International Development (USAID). In Ghana, she was the Acting Director of a USAID nationwide education project for primary-aged children. In Guatemala, she was the college counselor for three years at Colegio Maya, the American school in Guatemala City. She graduated from Dalhousie University in Halifax, Nova Scotia with a Bachelor's degree in Philosophy and English, from Smith College with a Master's degree in Education of the Deaf and from the University of Virginia with a Doctorate in Communications and Marketing.

Robin Joy Orlansky began her overseas experiences at the age of 3, when her father received a Fulbright Fellowship as a visiting professor, and the whole family moved to the former Yugoslavia. After returning to the USA for about 6 years, she returned overseas in 1989, when her father joined the Foreign Service. She accompanied her parents to Indonesia, Ghana, and Guatemala, where she graduated from Colegio Maya. She went on to graduate from the University of Chicago in 2001, with a concentration in East Asian Studies, and is currently living in Japan, where she teaches English to middle school-aged students.

Steven C. Rice has been posted abroad to the U.S. Interests Section in Havana, Cuba (1995–97) and the U.S. Embassy in Damascus, Syria (98–2000), where he met his wife, Rita. The couple currently live in Washington, D.C., where Steve worked in the Operations Center from 2000–2001 and is currently the political-military officer in Israel and Palestinian Affairs. Before joining the Foreign Service, Steve worked as a legislative assistant on Capitol Hill. A native of Wyoming, he holds an M.A. from Northwestern University in political science, a Master of International Management from the American Graduate School of International Management, and a B.A. in economics and French from the University of Wyoming.

Anne Allen Sullivan has taught in five different countries, in public and private schools, at levels ranging from kindergarten through university. Following her graduation from UCLA with a degree in English, she taught first grade at a private school in Newport Beach, CA. In 1991, Anne graduated from George Mason University's Foreign Affairs Spouse's Teacher Training Program (a teacher certification program). (She was in the first graduating class.) In Tegucigalpa, Honduras (1991–92), she taught elementary music. She taught first grade in Guatemala City (92–93); and in Santiago, Chile (93–95), Anne taught kindergarten. Upon returning to Washington for her husband's Korean language training, Anne completed her masters of education at

George Mason University. In Seoul, Korea (96–99), Anne taught Advanced Composition, English Literature, and freshman English at Sogang University. She also taught English for the Korean Ministry of Education. Anne, her husband, John, and their two daughters currently live in the Washington D.C. area, where Anne is the AAFSW Playgroup Coordinator.

Tamar Weisert graduated from the Jakarta International School in 1993. She went on to the Colorado College where she graduated in 1997 with a major in Anthropology and minor in Urban Studies. She spent several years during and after college working with troubled youth in Chicago, Guatemala City, Colorado, and Virginia. She is currently working part-time as a probation officer in Virginia, and full-time, with her husband Drake, raising their 15 month-old daughter, Lily. They are looking forward to joining the Foreign Service as soon as Drake is assigned to his A-100 class.

Terri Williams and her family have had over 30 years' experience making choices in the Foreign Service. Along the way, they lived in Tokyo, Japan; Kingston, Jamaica; and Cairo, Egypt. Through living in those countries, she was exposed to many diverse ways that cultures confronted their life decisions. During many tours in Washington, she chose to work to enhance the Foreign Service lifestyle by working in the State Department's Family Liaison Office, once when it was in the developmental state and later in training and supporting the Community Liaison Office program. She worked in the State Department's Transition Center, formulating the family training program and later working with people leaving the Foreign Service who were making choices on their retirement. She has spoken and taught both within and outside the government. She chose to complete her undergraduate degree in Cultural Anthropology in Cairo, Egypt, and enhanced her skills at Georgetown University with certificates both in Training and in Organization Development. She now volunteers her expertise with the Associates of the American Foreign Service Worldwide (AAFSW) in addition to teaching Intermediate Leadership Skills training to Foreign Service Officers. She and her husband Dennis have raised two incredible boys who have benefited greatly from their Foreign Service experiences.

Resources

Organizations and Websites

AAFSW (Associates of the American Foreign Service Worldwide, formerly the Association of American Foreign Service Women). The sponsor of this book, AAFSW is an independent, nonprofit organization that has been representing Foreign Service spouses, employees and retirees since 1960. Its current activities in Washington include a foreign-born spouses' group, a playgroup for parents with young children, the Evacuee Support Network, the annual Bookfair and speakers' programs.

AAFSW's website (**www.aafsw.org**) offers extensive information and resources, including Livelines, an e-mail discussion forum for Foreign Service, employees, family members and recruits (those who have passed the oral examination).

5125 MacArthur Blvd. NW, Suite 36
Washington, D.C. 20016
(202) 362–6514
www.aafsw.org

AFSA (American Foreign Service Association). Established in 1924, AFSA is the Foreign Service's official bargaining unit. It publishes the monthly *Foreign Service Journal* and advocates for members of the Foreign Service on a wide range of issues.

2101 E Street NW
Washington, D.C. 20037
(800) 704-AFSA; **www.afsa.org**

American Diplomacy. An online journal written and edited by current and former U.S. diplomats and sometimes spouses. Has a "Life in the Foreign Service" section as well as policy articles: **www. americandiplomacy.org**

Career In Your Suitcase. A website and book by British expatriate author Joanna Parfitt, focused on careers for accompanying spouses: **www.career-in-your-suitcase.com**

Expat Exchange. Offers online discussion and support communities for all categories of expatriates: **www.expatexchange.com**

Expat Expert. Expatriate-related news, views and links from Canadian diplomatic spouse, author and speaker Robin Pascoe: **www. expatexpert.com**

FAST-TRAIN Program. Helps spouses of foreign affairs professionals gain quick certification in order to work as teachers abroad.
Graduate School of Education MS 4B3
George Mason University
Fairfax, VA 22030–4444
(703) 993–3689/3688

Foreignservice.org. An unofficial resource and bulletin board.

Foreignservicecareers.gov. The State Department's new recruiting website.

Foreign Service Youth Foundation. With support from the FLO and AAFSW, the group sponsors the Foreign Service teen group AWAL (Around the World in a Lifetime) and preteen group Globe Trotters in Washington. It also offers books of interest to internationally-mobile families.
P.O. Box 39185
Washington, D.C. 20016, **www.fsyf.org**

GLIFAA. Gays and Lesbians in Foreign Affairs Agencies USA. Founded in 1992 to provide support and advocacy for gay and lesbian employees and their partners: **www.glifaa.org**.

The Idealist. A website listing thousands of non-profit organizations and jobs all over the world, of possible interest to job-seeking Foreign Service spouses: **www.idealist.org**

National Military Family Association
   2500 N. Van Dorn Street, Suite 102
   Alexandria, Virginia 22302–1601, **www.nmfa.org**

Tales from a Small Planet. A website created by Foreign Service spouses (formerly the "Spouses' Underground Newsletter," SUN). Offers honest, firsthand "Real Post Reports" describing daily life at posts around the world, most contributed by Foreign Service Officers and family members. Also includes literary and humorous reflections on overseas life, a comprehensive international schools list, and popular e-mail discussion groups and message boards, some focused on the Foreign Service: **www.talesmag.com or www.realpostreports.com**

TCK World. Information and links for "third-culture kids" and their families: **www.tckworld.com**

U.S. Department of State Resources (see www.state.gov)

The **Family Liaison Office (FLO)** works to improve the quality of life for FS officers and families, through the Community Liaison Office program and support with issues such as spouse employment, raising children abroad, schooling options, special-needs children, family crisis support, and naturalization of foreign-born spouses: **www.state.gov/m/dghr/flo**

The **Transition Center** includes the **Overseas Briefing Center (OBC),** the Transition Training Center and the Career Transition Center. The OBC offers employees and family members a wide range of information on overseas posts, as well as numerous courses and workshops: **www.state.gov/m/fsi/obc**

The **Office of Overseas Schools** helps Foreign Service families find out about and contact suitable schools overseas: **www.state.gov/m/a/os**

The **Employee Consultation Service** (ECS) offers State Department staff and families free counseling on personal or professional issues, including marital problems, grief, anxiety and children's needs: (202) 663–1815 ; **MEDECS@state.gov**

Books

Adams, John W. *U.S. Expatriate Handbook: Guide to Living & Working Abroad.* West Virginia University College of Business and Economics, 1998.

Bauer, Maria. *Beyond the Chestnut Trees.* Viking Press, 1986. The memoir of a foreign-born Foreign Service spouse returning to Prague after forty years away.

Bell, Linda. *Hidden Immigrants: Legacies of Growing Up Abroad.* Notre Dame, Indiana: Cross Cultural Publications, 1997. Honest reports from people who grew up as children abroad, collected by a Foreign Service spouse and journalist.

Bender, Margaret. *Foreign At Home and Away: Foreign-Born Wives in the U.S. Foreign Service.* New York: Writers Club Press, 2002. Personal case studies of 40 foreign-born wives of U.S. Foreign Service Officers.

Black, J. Stewart and Hal B. Gregersen. *So You're Going Overseas.* San Diego: Global Business Publishers, 1998. Accompanying workbooks for employees, spouses, kids and teenagers are also offered.

Blohm, Judith M. *Where in the World Are You Going?* Yarmouth, Maine: Intercultural Press, 1996.

Eakin, Kay Branaman. *According to My Passport, I'm Coming Home.* Washington, D.C.: Family Liaison Office, Department of State, 1998. A re-entry discussion focused on U.S. Foreign Service teens.

Education Options for Foreign Service Family Members, Washington, D.C.: Family Liaison Office, Department of State, 1996.

Employment Options for Foreign Service Family Members, Washington, D.C.: Family Liaison Office, Department of State, 2001.

Fenzi, Jewell, with Carl L. Nelson. *Married to the Foreign Service: An Oral History of the American Diplomatic Spouse.* Twayne Publishers, 1994. May be ordered from AAFSW.

Frew, Barbara. *Personal Finance for Overseas Americans: How to Direct Your Own Financial Future While Living Abroad.* GIL Financial Press, 2000.

Gregerson, Hal B. and J. Stewart Black. *So You're Coming Home.* San Diego: Global Business Publishers, 1999.

Hess, Melissa and Patricia Linderman. *The Expert Expatriate: Your Guide to Successful Relocation Abroad.* Yarmouth, Maine: Nicholas Brealey Intercultural Press, 2002. A guidebook written by the editors of this volume. See **www.expatguide.info**.

Hughes, Katherine L. *The Accidental Diplomat: Dilemmas of the Trailing Spouse.* Putnam Valley, New York: Aletheia Publications, 1998. A book on the role of Foreign Service spouses abroad, by the daughter of Patricia Hughes, a contributor to this volume.

Huw, Francis and Michelyne Callan. *Live and Work Abroad: A Guide for Modern Nomads.* Oxford, U.K.: Vacation Work Publications, 2001.

Inside a U.S. Embassy: How the Foreign Service Works for America. New January 2003 edition. American Foreign Service Association (AFSA), **www.afsa.org**.

Jehle-Caitcheon, Ngaire. *Parenting Abroad.* Putnam Valley, N.Y.: Aletheia Publications, 2003.

Kohls, L. Robert. *Survival Kit for Overseas Living.* 3rd ed. Yarmouth, Maine: Intercultural Press, 1996.

Maxfield, Brenda. *Up, Up and Away! A guide for children and their parents who are moving from one culture to another.* Washington, D.C.: Foreign Service Youth Foundation, 2001. An interactive book for elementary-age children. See **www.fsyf.org**.

McCluskey, Karen C., ed. *Notes from a Traveling Childhood: Readings for Internationally Mobile Parents and Children.* Washington, D.C.: Foreign Service Youth Foundation, 1994. See **www.fsyf.org**.

Parfitt, Joanna. *A Career in Your Suitcase: Finding the Perfect Portable Career.* New edition. Stamford, England: Summertime Publishing, 2002. See **www.career-in-your-suitcase.com**.

Parker, Elisabeth and Katherine Rumrill-Teece. *Here Today There Tomorrow: A Training Manual for Working with Internationally Mobile Youth.* Washington, D.C.: Foreign Service Youth Foundation, 2001. See **www.fsyf.org**.

Pascoe, Robin. *Culture Shock! Successful Living Abroad: A Wife's Guide.* Singapore: Times Editions, 1993.

Pascoe, Robin. *Culture Shock! Successful Living Abroad: A Parent's Guide.* Singapore: Times Editions, 1993.

Pascoe, Robin. *Homeward Bound: A Spouse's Guide to Repatriation.* Expatriate Press, 2000. See **www.expatriatepress.com**.

Pascoe, Robin. *A Moveable Marriage.* Vancouver, B.C.: Expatriate Press, 2003. See **www.expatriatepress.com**.

Piet-Pelon, Nancy J., and Barbara Hornby. *Women's Guide to Overseas Living,* 2nd ed. Yarmouth, Maine: Intercultural Press, 1992.

Pollock, David C. and Ruth E. Van Reken. *Third Culture Kids: The Experience of Growing Up Among Worlds.* Yarmouth, Maine: Intercultural Press, 1999.

Roman, Beverly D. *Footsteps Around the World: Relocation Tips for Teens.* Wilmington, N.C.: BR Anchor Publishing, 1999. See **www.branchor.com**.

Roman, Beverly D. *Let's Move Overseas: The International Edition of Let's Make A Move!* Wilmington, N.C.: BR Anchor Publishing, 1999. See **www.branchor.com**.

Romano, Dugan. *Intercultural Marriage: Promises and Pitfalls.* 2d ed. Yarmouth, Maine: Intercultural Press, 1997.

Schmiel, Gene and Kathryn Schmiel. *Welcome Home: Who Are You? Tales of a Foreign Service Family.* Putnam Valley, New York: Aletheia Publications, 1998.

Shepard, Steven. *Managing Cross-Cultural Transition.* Putnam Valley, New York: Aletheia Publications, 1997.

Smith, Carolyn D. *The Absentee American.* Putnam Valley, New York: Aletheia Publications, 1991, 1994. A study of over 300 returnees to the United States by an author who grew up in the Foreign Service.

Smith, Carolyn D. *Strangers at Home: Essays on the Effects of Living Overseas and Coming "Home" to a Strange Land.* Putnam Valley, New York: Aletheia Publications, 1996.

Storti, Craig. *The Art of Coming Home.* Yarmouth, Maine: Intercultural Press, 1997.

Storti, Craig. *The Art of Crossing Cultures.* Yarmouth, Maine: Intercultural Press, 1990.

Taber, Sara Mansfield. *Of Many Lands: Journal of a Traveling Childhood.* Washington, D.C.: Foreign Service Youth Foundation, 1997. See **www.fsyf.org**.

Wertsch, Mary Edwards. *Military Brats: Legacies of Childhood Inside the Fortress.* Putnam Valley, New York: Aletheia Publications, 1991, 1996.

About the Editors

Patricia Linderman is a writer, translator and Associate Editor of Tales from a Small Planet, **www.talesmag.com**. She has lived as a Foreign Service family member in Trinidad, Chile, Cuba and Germany.

Melissa Brayer Hess is a writer, teacher and founder of AAFSW's website, **www.aafsw.org**. She has lived in France, Nigeria, Russia, Algeria, Egypt, and Ukraine.

Melissa and Patricia have also co-authored the guidebook The Expert Expatriate: Your Guide to Successful Relocation Abroad (2002, Nicholas Brealey / Intercultural Press).

0-595-25077-7

Printed in the United States
82996LV00003B/109-156/A